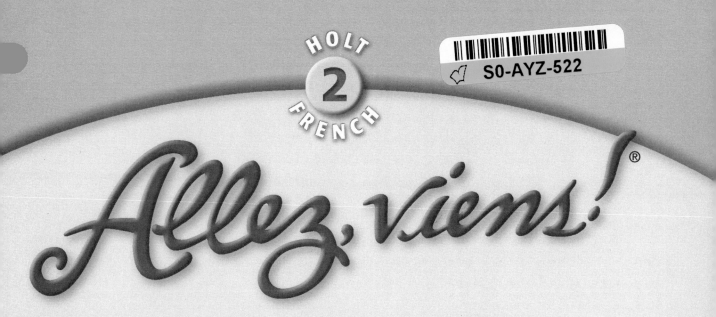

HOLT

2

FRENCH

Allez, viens!®

Student Make-Up
Assignments

HOLT, RINEHART AND WINSTON

A Harcourt Classroom Education Company

Austin · New York · Orlando · Atlanta · San Francisco · Boston · Dallas · Toronto · London

Contributing Writers

Dr. Cherie Mitschke
Southwestern University

Cover Photo Credits

(tl), Tim Haske/Index Stock; (tr), Network Productions/Index Stock (b) Digital imagery® © 2003 Photodisc, Inc.

Art Credits

All art, unless otherwise noted, by Holt, Rinehart & Winston.
Page 138, Bruce Roberts.

ALLEZ, VIENS! is a trademark licensed to Holt, Rinehart and Winston, registered in the United States of America and/or other jurisdictions.

Printed in the United States of America

ISBN 0-03-065681-8

1 2 3 4 5 6 7 066 05 04 03 02 01

Table of Contents

ANSWERS

Holt French 2 Allez, viens!

To the Teacher

The blackline masters in this ancillary will help you keep track of the instructional material covered in a school year, so that you can give make-up information to students who missed class.

The first section of the book is a Diagnostic Table. In the first column of the table is a list of all the major presentations that make up the building blocks of the **Chapitre:** the functional expressions, the grammar, and the vocabulary. The activities listed in the other four columns are correlated to the **Grammaire supplémentaire** in the *Pupil's Edition,* the **Cahier d'activités,** the **Travaux pratiques de grammaire,** and the **Interactive CD-ROM Tutor.** This table, which gives you an overview of the presentations and opportunities for practice, can also be used as a global reference for students who need extra practice in problem areas.

The second section of the book contains the Student Make-Up Assignments Checklists. These blackline masters (one for each **étape** of the *Pupil's Edition*) can be photocopied and given to students as make-up assignments. On the left-hand side of each blackline master is a list of the presentations in each **étape.** If students missed a specific presentation (or presentations), the checklist tells them what activities they can do in the **Grammaire supplémentaire** in the *Pupil's Edition,* the **Cahier d'activités,** the **Travaux pratiques de grammaire,** or the **Interactive CD-ROM Tutor** to practice the material they missed when they were absent from class.

The third section of the book contains Alternative Quizzes that can be given to students who were absent from class when the regular Grammar and Vocabulary Quiz (Quiz A in the Testing Program) was given. The Alternative Quizzes could also be used in a different way: You can give both quizzes in the regular class, alternating rows, for example, so that students are not tempted to glance at their neighbor's paper.

The Alternative Quizzes were carefully built to reflect the same weight and level of difficulty as the regular quizzes, so that you can be assured that two students who take different versions of the quiz feel that they have been tested equally.

Diagnostic Information

The activities listed in this table are taken from the the **Grammaire supplémentaire** in the *Pupil's Edition,* the **Cahier d'activités,** the **Travaux pratiques de grammaire,** and the **Interactive CD-ROM Tutor.** They provide students with extra practice in problem areas.

Grammaire = white background; **Vocabulaire** = light gray; **Comment dit-on... ?** = dark gray

CHAPITRE 1	Grammaire supplémentaire	Travaux pratiques de grammaire	Cahier d'activités	Interactive CD-ROM Tutor
Describing and characterizing yourself and others			Act. 3, p. 2	Act. 1, CD 1
The verbs **avoir** and **être**	Acts. 1–2, p. 24	Acts. 1–2, p. 1	Act. 4, p. 2	
Adjective agreement	Acts. 3–4, p. 24–25	Acts. 3–5, pp. 2–3	Act. 5, p. 3	Act. 2, CD 1
Expressing likes, dislikes, and preferences			Acts. 6–7, pp. 3–4	
The interrogative adjective **quel**	Act. 6, p. 25	Act. 6, p. 4		
Asking for information			Acts. 8–9, p. 4	Act. 3, CD 1
Vocabulaire: pour mon voyage, il me faut...		Acts. 8–10, p. 5	Acts. 10–11, p. 5	Act. 4, CD 1
The present tense forms and the past participle of -**ir** verbs	Acts. 7–8, p. 26	Acts. 11–13, pp. 6–7	Act. 13, p. 6	
Asking for and giving advice			Act. 15, p. 7	
Informal commands	Act. 9, p. 27	Acts. 14–15, pp. 7–8	Act. 14, p. 6	
Asking for, making, and responding to suggestions			Acts. 17–18, p. 8	Act. 5, CD 1
Relating a series of events			Acts. 20–21, p. 9	
Aller + infinitive	Acts. 10–11, p. 27	Acts. 20–23, pp. 10–11	Act. 19, p. 9	Act. 6, CD 1
CHAPITRE 2	Grammaire supplémentaire	Travaux pratiques de grammaire	Cahier d'activités	Interactive CD-ROM Tutor
Welcoming someone and responding to someone's welcome			Act. 2, p. 14	
The usage of **tu** and **vous**	Acts. 1–2, p. 52	Acts. 1–2, p. 12	Act. 3, p. 14	
Asking how someone is feeling and telling how you are feeling			Acts. 4–6, pp. 14–15	Act. 1, CD 1
Using intonation in yes-no questions and **est-ce que**	Acts. 3–4, p. 52	Acts. 3–4, p. 13		
Vocabulaire: la maison d'Antoine Morel		Acts. 5–6, p. 14	Acts. 7–9, pp. 16–17	Act. 2, CD 1
Pointing out where things are			Act. 10, p. 17	Act. 3, CD 1
Adjectives that precede the noun	Acts. 6–7, pp. 53–54	Acts. 9–10, p. 16	Acts. 11–12, pp. 17–18	Act. 4, CD 1
Paying and responding to compliments			Act. 14, p. 19	
Vocabulaire: places		Acts. 11–13, pp. 17–18	Act. 17, p. 20	Act. 5, CD 1
The usage of contractions with the preposition **à**	Acts. 8–10, p. 54–55	Acts. 14–16, pp. 18–19	Act. 18, p. 20	
Asking for and giving directions			Acts. 20–23, pp. 21–22	Act. 6, CD 1

CHAPITRE 3	Grammaire supplémentaire	Travaux pratiques de grammaire	Cahier d'activités	Interactive CD-ROM Tutor
Making purchases			Acts. 2–3, p. 26	
The usage of the pronoun **en**	Acts. 1–2, p. 82	Acts. 4–5, pp. 21–22	Acts. 4–5, pp. 26–27	
Vocabulaire: stores		Acts. 6–10, pp. 22–23	Acts. 8–10, p. 28	Act. 1, CD 1
Vocabulaire: meals and the different food		Acts. 11–12, p. 24	Acts. 11–12, p. 29	Act. 2, CD 1
Asking for, offering, accepting, and refusing food; paying and responding to compliments			Acts. 13–14, pp. 29–30	Act. 3, CD 1
The usage of the partitif	Acts. 6–7, p. 84	Acts. 15–16, p. 26	Acts. 15–16, p. 30	Act. 4, CD 1
Asking for and giving advice			Act. 20, p. 32	
The indirect object pronouns **lui** and **leur**	Acts. 8–9, p. 85	Acts. 17–18, p. 27	Act. 21, p. 32	Act. 5, CD 1
Vocabulaire: more stores		Acts. 19–21, p. 28	Acts. 23–25, pp. 33–34	Act. 6, CD 1
Extending good wishes			Acts. 26–27, p. 34	

CHAPITRE 4	Grammaire supplémentaire	Travaux pratiques de grammaire	Cahier d'activités	Interactive CD-ROM Tutor
Vocabulaire: places in Martinique		Acts. 1–3, pp. 29–30	Acts. 3–4, p. 38	Act. 1, CD 1
Asking for information and describing a place			Acts. 6–7, p. 39	
Vocabulaire: things to do on vacation		Acts. 5–7, pp. 31–32	Acts. 9–10, p. 41	Act. 2, CD 1
Reflexive verbs	Act. 3, p. 117			
Asking for and making suggestions			Acts. 11–13, p. 42	
Emphazing likes and dislikes			Act. 14, p. 43	Act. 3, CD 1
Different forms of the reflexive pronoun		Act. 8, p. 32		
The relative pronouns **ce qui** and **ce que**	Acts. 4–6, p. 117	Acts. 9–10, p. 33		
Vocabulaire: reflexive verbs		Acts. 11–12, p. 34		
Relating a series of events			Acts. 16–17, p. 44	Act. 4, CD 1
The present tense of reflexive verbs	Acts. 7–9, pp. 118–119	Acts. 13–15, pp. 35–36	Acts. 18–21, pp. 45–46	Act. 5, CD 1
The usage of adverbs of frequency	Act. 10, p. 119	Act. 16, p. 36		

CHAPITRE 5	Grammaire supplémentaire	Travaux pratiques de grammaire	Cahier d'activités	Interactive CD-ROM Tutor
Vocabulaire: the daily routing in the past		Acts. 1–4, pp. 37–38	Acts. 2–5, pp. 50–51	Act. 1, CD 2
Expressing concern for someone			Act. 7, p. 51	
The **passé composé**	Acts. 1–4, pp. 148–149	Acts. 5–8, pp. 39–40	Acts. 8–9, p. 52	Act. 2, CD 2
Inquiring; expressing satisfaction and frustration		Acts. 9–10, p. 41	Acts. 11–12, p. 53	Act. 3, CD 2
Introduction to the **passé composé** with **être**	Acts. 5–9, pp. 149–151	Acts. 11–14, pp. 42–43	Acts. 13–14, pp. 53–54	Act. 4, CD 2
Sympathizing with and consoling someone			Acts. 16–17, p. 55	Act. 5, CD 2
Giving reasons and making excuses			Acts. 19–21, p. 56	
Congratulating and reprimanding someone	Act. 10, p. 151	Acts. 15–17, p. 44	Acts. 22–23, pp. 57–58	Act. 6, CD 2

CHAPITRE 6	Grammaire supplémentaire	Travaux pratiques de grammaire	Cahier d'activités	Interactive CD-ROM Tutor
Vocabulaire: weekend activities		Acts. 1–4, pp. 45–46	Acts. 3–4, pp. 62–63	Act. 1, CD 2
Asking for opinions; expressing enthusiasm, indifferences, and dissatisfaction			Acts. 7–8, p. 64	Act. 2, CD 2
Imperfect form of **être**: c'était	Act. 3, p. 177	Act. 5, p. 46		
Vocabulaire: **être** verbs		Acts. 6–10, pp. 47–49	Acts. 10–11, p. 65	Act. 3, CD 2
The **passé composé** with **être**	Acts. 5 and 8, pp. 177–178	Acts. 11–13, pp. 49–50	Acts. 12–13, p. 66	Act. 4, CD 2
Expressing disbelief and doubt			Act. 15, p. 67	
Asking for and giving information			Acts. 17–19, pp. 68–69	Act. 5, CD 2
Formal questions	Act. 10, p. 179	Acts. 14–15, p. 51	Act. 20, p. 69	Act. 6, CD 2
The verb **ouvrir**	Act. 11, p. 179	Acts. 16–17, p. 52	Act. 21, p. 69	

CHAPITRE 7	Grammaire supplémentaire	Travaux pratiques de grammaire	Cahier d'activités	Interactive CD-ROM Tutor
Expressing concern for someone; complaining			Act. 3, p. 74	
Vocabulaire: illnesses		Acts. 1–2, p. 53	Acts. 4–5, p. 74	
Vocabulaire: parts of the body		Acts. 3–5, pp. 54–55	Acts. 6–7, p. 75	
Vocabulaire: accidents		Act. 6, p. 55		Act. 1, CD 2
Reflexive verbs	Acts. 2–3, pp. 206–207	Acts. 7–8, p. 56	Act. 8, p. 76	Act. 2, CD 2
Vocabulaire: exercising		Acts. 9–11, p. 57	Act. 11, p. 77	Act. 3, CD 2
The pronoun **en**	Acts. 4–5, pp. 207–208	Acts. 13–14, pp. 58–59		
Giving advice, accepting, and rejecting advice			Acts. 13–14, p. 78	
The verb **devoir**	Act. 6, p. 208	Act. 15, p. 59		
Expressing discouragement and offering encouragement			Acts. 16–17, p. 79	Act. 4, CD 2
Vocabulaire: eating right		Acts. 16–17, p. 60	Act. 18, p. 80	Act. 5, CD 2
The verb **se nourrir**	Act. 8, p. 209	Acts. 18–19, p. 61	Act. 21, p. 81	
Justifying your recommendations; advising against something			Acts. 22–23, pp. 81–82	Act. 6, CD 2
CHAPITRE 8	Grammaire supplémentaire	Travaux pratiques de grammaire	Cahier d'activités	Interactive CD-ROM Tutor
Telling what or whom you miss; reassuring someone			Acts. 3–5, p. 86	
Asking and telling what things were like	Act. 1, p. 240			
Vocabulaire: describing things		Acts. 1–4, pp. 62–63	Acts. 6–7, p. 87	Act. 1, CD 2
The imperfect of **être** and **avoir**	Acts. 2–3, p. 240	Acts. 5–6, p. 64	Act. 8, p. 88	Act. 2, CD 2
Vocabulaire: Describing things in the past		Acts. 7–10, pp.65–66	Acts. 10–11, p. 89	
Reminiscing				Act. 3, CD 2
The imperfect	Acts. 4–7, pp. 241–242	Acts. 11–15, pp. 67–68	Acts. 13–15, pp. 90–91	Act. 4, CD 2
Vocabulaire: souvenirs		Acts. 16–17, p. 69	Acts. 16–18, pp. 92–93	Acts. 5–6, CD 2
Making and responding to suggestions			Acts. 19–21, pp. 93–94	
Making suggestions with the imperfect	Acts. 8–10, p. 243	Acts. 18–19, p. 70		

Holt French 2 Allez, viens!

CHAPITRE 9	Grammaire supplémentaire	Travaux pratiques de grammaire	Cahier d'activités	Interactive CD-ROM Tutor
Vocabulaire: moods and emotions		Acts. 1–3, pp. 71–72	Acts. 3–5, p. 98	Act. 1, CD 3
The imperfect and the expression **avoir l'air**	Acts. 1–3, pp. 272–273	Acts. 4–5, p. 72		
Wondering what happened; offering possible explanations; accepting or rejecting explanations			Acts. 6–8, pp. 99–100	Act. 2, CD 3
Vocabulaire: explaining		Acts. 6–7, p. 73	Acts. 10–12, pp. 101–102	Act. 3, CD 3
Breaking some news; showing interest			Act. 13, p. 102	
The **passé composé** vs. the **imparfait**	Acts. 4–9, pp. 274–275	Acts. 8–12, pp. 74–76	Act. 14, p. 103	Act. 4, CD 3
Beginning, continuing, and ending a story			Acts. 16–17, p. 104	Act. 5, CD 3
More of the **passé composé** vs. the **imparfait**, and the usage of the phrase **en train de**	Acts. 8–9, p. 275	Acts. 13–14, p. 77	Acts. 18–20, pp. 105–106	Act. 6, CD 3

CHAPITRE 10	Grammaire supplémentaire	Travaux pratiques de grammaire	Cahier d'activités	Interactive CD-ROM Tutor
Sharing a confidence			Act. 3, p. 110	
Asking for and giving advice			Acts. 4–5, pp. 110–111	Act. 1, CD 3
Vocabulaire: giving advice		Acts. 1–4, pp. 78–80		Act. 2, CD 3
Object pronouns and their placement	Acts. 1–6, pp. 300–301	Acts. 5–7, pp. 80–81	Act. 8, p. 112	Act. 3, CD 3
Asking for and granting a favor; making excuses			Act. 11, p. 114	
Vocabulaire: preparing a party		Acts. 8–10, pp. 82–83	Act. 12, p. 114	Act. 4, CD 3
The usage of the direct object pronouns in the **passé composé**	Acts. 7–10, pp. 302–303	Acts. 11–14, pp. 84–85	Acts. 14–15, p. 115	Act. 5, CD 3
Apologizing and accepting an apology; reproaching someone			Acts. 16–18, pp. 116–117	Act. 6, CD 3
The usage of the pronouns with infinitives	Acts. 11–12, p. 303	Acts. 15–16, p. 86	Act. 19, p. 117	

CHAPITRE 11	Grammaire supplémentaire	Travaux pratiques de grammaire	Cahier d'activités	Interactive CD-ROM Tutor
Identifying people and things			Act. 2, p. 122	
The verb **connaître**	Act. 1, p. 330	Acts. 1–2, pp. 87–88	Act. 3, p. 122	
Vocabulaire: entertainment		Acts. 3–4, p. 88	Act. 4, p. 123	
Il/Elle est... vs. **C'est...**	Acts. 2–4, pp. 330–331	Acts. 5–7, p. 89	Act. 6, p. 123	Act. 1, CD 3
Vocabulaire: music		Acts. 8–11, pp. 90–91	Acts. 7–8, p. 124	Act. 2, CD 3
Asking for and giving information			Acts. 10–11, pp. 125–126	Act. 3, CD 3
Vocabulaire: movies		Acts. 12–15, pp. 92–93	Acts. 12–13, pp. 126–127	
Giving opinions			Act. 15, p. 128	
Vocabulaire: books		Acts. 16–18, pp. 94–95	Act. 16, p. 128	Act. 4, CD 3
Summarizing			Act. 20, p. 129	Act. 5, CD 3
The relative pronouns **qui** and **que**	Acts. 5–7, pp. 332–333	Acts. 19–21, pp. 96–97	Acts. 21–22, p. 130	Act. 6, CD 3
CHAPITRE 12	Grammaire supplémentaire	Travaux pratiques de grammaire	Cahier d'activités	Interactive CD-ROM Tutor
Asking for and giving information; giving directions			Acts. 2–4, pp. 134–135	Act. 1, CD 3
Vocabulaire: animals		Acts. 1–3, p. 98	Act. 5, p. 135	Act. 2, CD 3
Vocabulaire: things to do		Acts. 4–6, p. 99	Act. 6, p. 136	
Vocabulaire: camping		Acts. 7–8, pp. 100–101	Acts. 8–9, p. 137	Act. 3, CD 3
The verb **emporter**	Acts. 4–5, pp. 365–366	Acts. 10–11, p. 102		
Complaining; expressing discouragement and offering encouragement			Act. 11, p. 138	Act. 4, CD 3
Vocabulaire: rules		Acts. 12–14, p. 103	Act. 12, p. 139	
Asking for and giving advice			Act. 13, p. 139	
Relating a series of events; describing people and places			Acts. 15–16, p. 140	Act. 5, CD 3
The **passé composé** and the **imparfait**	Acts. 6–9, pp. 366–367	Acts. 15–20, pp. 104–107	Acts. 17–19, pp. 140–142	Act. 6, CD 3

STUDENT MAKE-UP ASSIGNMENTS CHECKLIST

Nom_____ Classe_____ Date_____

1 Bon séjour!

■ PREMIERE ETAPE Student Make-Up Assignments Checklist

Pupil's Edition, pp. 9–12

Study the expressions in the **Comment dit-on... ?** box on page 9: describing and characterizing yourself and others. You should know how to describe and characterize yourself and others.	☐ For additional practice, do Activity 3, p. 2 in the **Cahier d'activités.** ☐ For additional practice, do Activity 1, CD 1 in the **Interactive CD-ROM Tutor.**
Study the grammar presentation in the **Grammaire** box on page 10: the verbs **avoir** and **être.**	☐ Do Activity 7, p. 10 as a writing activity. ☐ Do Activity 11, p. 12 as a writing activity. ☐ For additional practice, do Activities 1–2, p. 24 in the **Grammaire supplémentaire.** ☐ For additional practice, do Activity 4, p. 2 in the **Cahier d'activités.** ☐ For additional practice, do Activities 1–2, p.1 in the **Travaux pratiques de grammaire.**
Study the grammar presentation in the **Grammaire** box on page 11: adjective agreement.	☐ Do Activity 8, p. 11 as a writing activity. ☐ For additional practice, do Activities 3–4, pp. 24–25 in the **Grammaire supplémentaire.** ☐ For additional practice, do Activity 5, p. 3 in the **Cahier d'activités.** ☐ For additional practice, do Activities 3–5, pp. 2–3 in the **Travaux pratiques de grammaire.** ☐ For additional practice, do Activity 2, CD 1 in the **Interactive CD-ROM Tutor.**
Study the expressions in the **Comment dit-on... ?** box on page 11: expressing likes, dislikes, and preferences. You should know how to say what you and others like, dislike, and prefer.	☐ Do Activity 10, p. 12. ☐ For additional practice, do Activities 6–7, pp. 3–4 in the **Cahier d'activités.**
Study the grammar presentation in the **Note de grammaire** box on page 12: the interrogative adjective **quel.**	☐ For additional practice, do Activity 6, p. 25 in the **Grammaire supplémentaire.** ☐ For additional practice, do Activity 6, p. 4 in the **Travaux pratiques de grammaire.**

Study the expressions in the **Comment dit-on... ?** box on page 12: asking for information. You should know how to ask for information.

☐ Do Activity 12, p. 12 as a writing activity. Write a make up interview between you and a famous person.

☐ For additional practice, do Activities 8–9, p. 4 in the **Cahier d'activités.**

☐ For additional practice, do Activity 3, CD 1 in the **Interactive CD-ROM Tutor.**

■ PREMIERE ETAPE Self-Test

Can you describe and characterize yourself and others?	How would you describe and characterize . . . 1. yourself? 2. your best friend? 3. a family member?
Can you express likes, dislikes, and preferences?	How would you say that you like the things in the pictures in Activity 2 on the **Que sais-je?** page 30? How would you say that you dislike them? That you prefer something else?
Can you ask for information?	How would you ask someone . . . 1. what he or she likes to do? 2. what sport he or she plays? 3. what type of music he or she likes? 4. what his or her favorite film is?

For an online self-test, go to **go.hrw.com**.

WA3 PARIS REGION-1

Holt French 2 Allez, viens!, Chapter 1

Nom _____ *Classe* _____ *Date* _____

Bon séjour!

■ DEUXIEME ETAPE Student Make-Up Assignments Checklist

Pupil's Edition, pp. 13–16

Study the **Vocabulaire** on page 14.	☐ For additional practice, do Activities 10–11, p. 5 in the **Cahier d'activités.**
	☐ For additional practice, do Activities 8–10, p. 5 in the **Travaux pratiques de grammaire.**
	☐ For additional practice, do Activity 4, CD 1 in the **Interactive CD-ROM Tutor.**
Study the grammar presentation in the **Note de grammaire** box on page 14: the present tense forms and the past participle of the –**ir** verbs.	☐ Do Activity 14, p. 14.
	☐ Do Activity 15, p. 15 as a writing activity. Describe your favorite activity.
	☐ For additional practice, do Activities 7–8, p. 26 in the **Grammaire supplémentaire.**
	☐ For additional practice, do Activity 13, p. 6 in the **Cahier d'activités.**
	☐ For additional practice, do Activities 11–13, pp. 6–7 in the **Travaux pratiques de grammaire.**
Study the expressions in the **Comment dit-on... ?** box on page 15: asking for and giving advice. You should know how to ask for and give advice.	☐ Do Activity 17, p. 15 as a writing activity.
	☐ For additional practice, do Activity 15, p. 7 in the **Cahier d'activités.**
Study the grammar presentation in the **Note de grammaire** box on page 15: commands.	☐ Do Activity 18, p. 16 as a writing activity.
	☐ Do Activity 19, p. 16 as a writing activity.
	☐ Do Activity 20, p. 16.
	☐ For additional practice, do Activity 9, p. 27 in the **Grammaire supplémentaire.**
	☐ For additional practice, do Activity 14, p. 6 in the **Cahier d'activités.**
	☐ For additional practice, do Activities 14–15, pp. 7–8 in the **Travaux pratiques de grammaire.**

■ DEUXIEME ETAPE Self-Test

Can you ask for and give advice?	How would you ask someone what to take on a trip?
	What would you advise a friend to bring to . . .
	1. the beach?
	2. the mountains in the winter?
	3. Chicago in the spring?

 For an online self-test, go to **go.hrw.com**.

WA3 PARIS REGION-1

CHAPITRE

1 Bon séjour!

■ TROISIEME ETAPE Student Make-Up Assignments Checklist

Pupil's Edition, pp. 18–21

Study the expressions in the **Comment dit-on... ?** box on page 18: asking for, making, and responding to suggestions. You should know how to ask for, make, and respond to suggestions.	☐ Do Activity 23, p. 19 as a writing activity. Write the conversation between you and your friend.
	☐ Do Activity 24, p. 19 as a writing activity. Write the conversation between you and your friends.
	☐ For additional practice, do Activities 17–18, p. 8 in the **Cahier d'activités**.
	☐ For additional practice, do Activity 5, CD 1 in the **Interactive CD-ROM Tutor**.
Study the expressions in the **Comment dit-on... ?** box on page 20: relating a series of events. You should know how to tell what happened in sequential order.	☐ Do Activity 26, p. 20 as a writing activity.
	☐ For additional practice, do Activities 20–21, p. 9 in the **Cahier d'activités**.
Study the grammar presentation in the **Note de grammaire** box on page 21: **aller** + infinitive.	☐ Do Activity 27, p. 21 as a writing activity.
	☐ Do Activity 28, p. 21.
	☐ For additional practice, do Activities 10–11, p. 27 in the **Grammaire supplémentaire**.
	☐ For additional practice, do Activity. 19, p. 9 in the **Cahier d'activités**.
	☐ For additional practice, do Activities 20–23, pp. 10–11 in the **Travaux pratiques de grammaire**.
	☐ For additional practice, do Activity 6, CD 1 in the **Interactive CD-ROM Tutor**.

CHAPITRE 1

■ TROISIEME ETAPE Self-Test

Can you ask for, make, and respond to suggestions?	How would you . . . 1. ask a friend what to do? 2. suggest that you can go shopping if your friend wants to? 3. suggest that you could play soccer? 4. ask your friend if he or she would like to go to the movies? How would you respond to the following suggestions if you agreed? If you disagreed? If you preferred to do something else? 1. On pourrait faire les magasins. 2. Tu as envie de regarder la télévision?
Can you relate a series of events?	How would your friend tell you that he or she is going to do the activities depicted in Activity 8 on the **Que sais-je?** page 30 in the order in which they appear?

 For an online self-test, go to **go.hrw.com**.

WA3 PARIS REGION-1

CHAPITRE 2

Bienvenue à Chartres!

■ PREMIERE ETAPE Student Make-Up Assignments Checklist

Pupil's Edition, pp. 37–40

Study the expressions in the **Comment dit-on... ?** box on page 37: welcoming someone and responding to someone's welcome. You should know how to welcome someone and how to respond to someone's welcome.	☐ For additional practice, do Activity 2, p. 14 in the **Cahier d'activités**.
Study the grammar presentation in the **Note de grammaire** box on page 38: the usage of **tu** and **vous**.	☐ Do Activity 8, p. 38 as a writing activity. ☐ For additional practice, do Activities 1–2, p. 52 in the **Grammaire supplémentaire**. ☐ For additional practice, do Activity 3, p. 14 in the **Cahier d'activités**. ☐ For additional practice, do Activities 1–2, p. 12 in the **Travaux pratiques de grammaire**.
Study the expressions in the **Comment dit-on... ?** box on page 38: asking how someone is feeling and telling how you are feeling. You should know how to ask how someone is feeling and tell how you are feeling.	☐ Do Activity 9, p. 38 as a writing activity. Write out the two parts that go together. ☐ For additional practice, do Activities 4–6, pp. 14–15 in the **Cahier d'activités**. ☐ For additional practice, do Activity 1, CD 1 in the **Interactive CD-ROM Tutor**.
Study the grammar presentation in the **Note de grammaire** box on page 38: using intonation in yes-no questions and **est-ce-que**.	☐ For additional practice, do Activities 3–4, p. 52 in the **Grammaire supplémentaire**. ☐ For additional practice, do Activities 3–4, p. 13 in the **Travaux pratiques de grammaire**.

CHAPITRE 2

■ PREMIERE ETAPE Self-Test

CHAPITRE 2

Can you welcome someone and respond to someone's welcome?	What would you say to welcome . . . 1. your pen pal Jean-Louis? 2. your mother's friend? How would you respond to your friend's father, who says . . . 1. Bienvenue chez nous. 2. Fais comme chez toi. 3. Tu as fait bon voyage?
Can you ask how someone is feeling and tell how you are feeling?	How would you ask Etienne if he's . . . 1. not too tired? 2. hungry? 3. thirsty? How would you say that you're . . . 1. fine? 2. very hungry? 3. a little thirsty?

For an online self-test, go to **go.hrw.com**.

WA3 PARIS REGION-2

CHAPITRE 2

Bienvenue à Chartres!

■ DEUXIEME ETAPE Student Make-Up Assignments Checklist

Pupil's Edition, pp. 40–44

Study the **Vocabulaire** on page 41.	☐ Do Activity 16, p. 42 as a writing activity.
	☐ For additional practice, do Activities 7–9, pp. 16–17 in the **Cahier d'activités.**
	☐ For additional practice, do Activities 5–6, p. 14 in the **Travaux pratiques de grammaire.**
	☐ For additional practice, do Activity 2, CD 1 in the **Interactive CD-ROM Tutor.**
Study the expressions in the **Comment dit-on... ?** box on page 43: pointing out where things are. You should know how to tell where something is.	☐ Do Activity 19, p. 43.
	☐ For additional practice, do Activity 10, p. 17 in the **Cahier d'activités.**
	☐ For additional practice, do Activity 3, CD 1 in the **Interactive CD-ROM Tutor.**
Study the grammar presentation in the **Grammaire** box on page 43: adjectives that precede the noun.	☐ Do Activity 20, p. 44.
	☐ Do Activity 21, p. 44.
	☐ For additional practice, do Activities 6–7, p. 53–54 in the **Grammaire supplémentaire.**
	☐ For additional practice, do Activities 11–12, pp. 17–18 in the **Cahier d'activités.**
	☐ For additional practice, do Activity 9–10, p. 16 in the **Travaux pratiques de grammaire.**
	☐ For additional practice, do Activity 4, CD 1 in the **Interactive CD-ROM Tutor.**
Study the expressions in the **Comment dit-on... ?** box on page 44: paying and responding to compliments. You should know how to pay a compliment and how to respond to one.	☐ Do Activity 23, p. 44 as a writing activity. Write the possible compliments your classmates would pay you.
	☐ Do Activity 24, p. 44.
	☐ For additional practice, do Activity 14, p. 19 in the **Cahier d'activités.**

CHAPITRE 2

■ DEUXIEME ETAPE Self-Test

Can you point out where things are?	When you're showing someone your home, how would you point out . . . 1. your room? 2. the bathroom? 3. the kitchen?
Can you pay and respond to compliments?	How would you compliment someone on the things in the pictures in Activity 6 on the **Que sais-je?** page 50? How would you respond to a compliment?

 For an online self-test, go to **go.hrw.com**.

WA3 PARIS REGION-2

CHAPITRE 2

CHAPITRE 2

Bienvenue à Chartres!

■ TROISIEME ETAPE Student Make-Up Assignments Checklist

Pupil's Edition, pp. 46–49

Study the **Vocabulaire** on page 47.	☐ For additional practice, do Activity 17, p. 20 in the **Cahier d'activités**.
	☐ For additional practice, do Activities 11–13, pp. 17–18 in the **Travaux pratiques de grammaire**.
	☐ For additional practice, do Activity 5, CD 1 in the **Interactive CD-ROM Tutor**.
Study the grammar presentation in the **Note de grammaire** box on page 48: usage of contractions with the preposition **à**.	☐ Do Activity 27, p. 48 as a writing activity.
	☐ Do Activity 28, p. 48 as a writing activity.
	☐ For additional practice, do Activities 8–10, pp. 54–55 in the **Grammaire supplémentaire**.
	☐ For additional practice, do Activity 18, p. 20 in the **Cahier d'activités**.
	☐ For additional practice, do Activities 14–16, pp. 18–19 in the **Travaux pratiques de grammaire**.
Study the expressions in the **Comment dit-on... ?** box on page 49: asking for and giving directions. You should know how to ask for and give directions.	☐ Do Activity 30, p. 49.
	☐ Do Activity 31, p. 49 as a writing activity. Pick a starting point and an ending point, then write down the directions of how to get there.
	☐ Do Activity 32, p. 49 as a writing activity.
	☐ For additional practice, do Activities 20–23, pp. 21–22 in the **Cahier d'activités**.
	☐ For additional practice, do Activity 6, CD 1 in the **Interactive CD-ROM Tutor**.

CHAPITRE 2

■ TROISIEME ETAPE Self-Test

Can you ask for and give directions?	How would you ask directions to . . .

How would you ask directions to . . .

1. the train station?
2. the post office?
3. the library?

How would you give someone directions from your school to . . .

1. your favorite fast-food restaurant?
2. the nearest movie theater?

For an online self-test, go to **go.hrw.com**.

WA3 PARIS REGION-2

CHAPITRE 2

CHAPITRE

3 Un repas à la française

■ PREMIERE ETAPE Student Make-Up Assignments Checklist

Pupil's Edition, pp. 65–68

Study the expressions in the **Comment dit-on... ?** box on page 66: making purchases. You should know how to make purchases.	☐ Do Activity 9, p. 66 as a writing activity. ☐ Do Activity 10, p. 66 as a writing activity. Write the shopping conversations. ☐ For additional practice, do Activities 2–3, p. 26 in the **Cahier d'activités.**
Study the grammar presentation in the **Note de grammaire** box on page 66: the object pronoun **en.**	☐ Do Activity 12, p. 68 as a writing activity. ☐ Do Activity 13, p. 68 as a writing activity. ☐ Do Activity 14, p. 68 as a writing activity. ☐ Do Activity 15, p. 68. ☐ For additional practice, do Activities 1–2, p. 82 in the **Grammaire supplémentaire.** ☐ For additional practice, do Activities 4–5, pp. 26–27 in the **Cahier d'activités.** ☐ For additional practice, do Activities 4–5, pp. 21–22 in the **Travaux pratiques de grammaire.**
Study the **Vocabulaire** on page 67.	☐ Do Activity 11, p. 68 as a writing activity. ☐ For additional practice, do Activities 8–10, p. 28 in the **Cahier d'activités.** ☐ For additional practice, do Activities 6–10, pp. 22–23 in the **Travaux pratiques de grammaire.** ☐ For additional practice, do Activity 1, CD 1 in the **Interactive CD-ROM Tutor.**

CHAPITRE 3

■ PREMIERE ETAPE Self-Test

Can you make purchases?	In France, how would you . . .
	1. ask how much the shrimp costs?
	2. ask for two kilograms of tomatoes?
	3. ask how much all your purchases cost?
	Where would you go to buy . . .
	1. a pastry?
	2. eggs?
	3. snails?
	4. ham?
	5. a chicken?
	6. a croissant?
	What would you expect to have for a typical French breakfast, lunch, and dinner?

 For an online self-test, go to **go.hrw.com**.

WA3 PARIS REGION-3

CHAPITRE 3

CHAPITRE

3 Un repas à la française

■ DEUXIEME ETAPE Student Make-Up Assignments Checklist

Pupil's Edition, pp. 70–73

Study the **Vocabulaire** on page 71.	☐ Do Activity 19, p. 71 as a writing activity.
	☐ Do Activity 21, p. 72.
	☐ For additional practice, do Activities 11–12, p. 29 in the **Cahier d'activités.**
	☐ For additional practice, do Activities 11–12, p. 24 in the **Travaux pratiques de grammaire.**
	☐ For additional practice, do Activity 2, CD 1 in the **Interactive CD-ROM Tutor.**
Study the expressions in the **Comment dit-on... ?** box on page 73: asking for, offering, accepting, and refusing food; paying and responding to compliments. You should know how to speak at the table.	☐ Do Activity 23, p. 73 as a writing activity.
	☐ Do Activity 24, p. 73 as a writing activity.
	☐ For additional practice, do Activities 13–14, pp. 29–30 in the **Cahier d'activités.**
	☐ For additional practice, do Activity 3, CD 1 in the **Interactive CD-ROM Tutor.**
Study the grammar presentation in the **Note de grammaire** box on page 73: usage of the partitive.	☐ Do Activity 25, p. 73.
	☐ Do Activity 26, p. 73 as a writing activity.
	☐ For additional practice, do Activities 6–7, p. 84 in the **Grammaire supplémentaire.**
	☐ For additional practice, do Activities 15–16, p. 30 in the **Cahier d'activités.**
	☐ For additional practice, do Activities 15–16, p. 26 in the **Travaux pratiques de grammaire.**
	☐ For additional practice, do Activity 4, CD 1 in the **Interactive CD-ROM Tutor.**

CHAPITRE 3

■ DEUXIEME ETAPE Self-Test

Can you ask for, offer, accept, and refuse food?	How would you . . . 1. ask for more of your favorite dessert? 2. ask someone to pass your favorite main dish? 3. offer someone something to drink? How would you respond if you were offered a second helping? 1. You'd like some more. 2. You just couldn't eat any more.
Can you pay and respond to compliments?	What would you say to compliment the meal you had just eaten? How would you respond to that compliment?

 For an online self-test, go to **go.hrw.com**.

WA3 PARIS REGION-3

CHAPITRE 3

Holt French 2 Allez, viens!, Chapter 3

CHAPITRE 3 Un repas à la française

■ TROISIEME ETAPE Student Make-Up Assignments Checklist

Pupil's Edition, pp. 75–79

Study the expressions in the **Comment dit-on... ?** box on page 76: asking for and giving advice. You should know how to ask for and give advice.	☐ For additional practice, do Activity 20, p. 32 in the **Cahier d'activités.**
Study the grammar presentation in the **Grammaire** box on page 76: the indirect object pronouns **lui** and **leur**.	☐ Do Activity 29, p. 77 as a writing activity. ☐ For additional practice, do Activities 8–9, p. 85 in the **Grammaire supplémentaire.** ☐ For additional practice, do Activity 21, p. 32 in the **Cahier d'activités.** ☐ For additional practice, do Activities 17–18, p. 27 in the **Travaux pratiques de grammaire.** ☐ For additional practice, do Activity 5, CD 1 in the **Interactive CD-ROM Tutor.**
Study the **Vocabulaire** on page 77.	☐ Do Activity 31, p. 78 as a writing activity. ☐ Do Activity 32, p. 78 as a writing activity. ☐ For additional practice, do Activities 23–25, pp. 33–34 in the **Cahier d'activités.** ☐ For additional practice, do Activities 19–21, p. 28 in the **Travaux pratiques de grammaire.** ☐ For additional practice, do Activity 6, CD 1 in the **Interactive CD-ROM Tutor.**
Study the expressions in the **Comment dit-on... ?** box on page 79: extending good wishes. You should know how to tell someone you wish them well.	☐ Do Activity 33, p. 79 as a writing activity. ☐ Do Activity 34, p. 79 as a writing activity. ☐ Do Activity 35, p. 79 as a writing activity. ☐ For additional practice, do Activities 26–27, p. 34 in the **Cahier d'activités.**

CHAPITRE 3

■ TROISIEME ETAPE Self-Test

Can you ask for and give advice?	How would you ask for advice about what to give someone for his or her birthday?
	How would you advise your friend to give his or her grandmother the gifts in the pictures in Activity 8 on the **Que sais-je?** page 88?
	At what stores would you buy the gifts in the previous activity?
	How would you respond to a gift idea if . . . 1. you didn't like the idea? 2. you did like the idea?
Can you extend good wishes?	What would you say to someone who is . . . 1. leaving by car on vacation? 2. having a birthday? 3. not feeling well?

 For an online self-test, go to **go.hrw.com**.

WA3 PARIS REGION-3

Holt French 2 Allez, viens!, Chapter 3

Nom_____ Classe_____ Date_____

4 Sous les tropiques

■ PREMIERE ETAPE Student Make-Up Assignments Checklist

Pupil's Edition, pp. 99–102

Study the **Vocabulaire** on page 100.	☐ Do Activity 7, p. 100 as a writing activity. Rewrite the sentences that are true, and fix the ones that are false.
	☐ Do Activity 9, p. 101 as a writing activity.
	☐ Do Activity 10, p. 101 as a writing activity.
	☐ Do Activity 11, p. 101 as a writing activity. Write the descriptions.
	☐ For additional practice, do Activities 3–4, p. 38 in the **Cahier d'activités**
	☐ For additional practice, do Activities 1–3, pp. 29–30 in the **Travaux pratiques de grammaire.**
	☐ For additional practice, do Activity 1, CD 1 in the **Interactive CD-ROM Tutor.**
Study the expressions in the **Comment dit-on... ?** box on page 102: asking for information and describing a place. You should know how to ask for information about a place and how to give it.	☐ Do Activity 12, p. 102.
	☐ Do Activity 14, p. 102.
	☐ Do Activity 15, p. 102 as a writing activity. Write the conversation.
	☐ For additional practice, do Activities 6–7, p. 39 in the **Cahier d'activités.**

CHAPITRE 4

■ PREMIERE ETAPE Self-Test

Can you ask for information?	How would you ask . . .
	1. the location of a place?
	2. what it's like?
	3. what attractions there are?
	4. what the weather is like?
Can you describe a place?	How would you describe the state where you live? Tell . . .
	1. where it's located.
	2. what's in the north, south, east, and west.
	3. how big it is in relation to others.
	4. what there is to do there.
	5. what there is to see there.

 For an online self-test, go to **go.hrw.com**.

WA3 MARTINIQUE-4

4 Sous les tropiques

■ DEUXIEME ETAPE Student Make-Up Assignments Checklist

Pupil's Edition, pp. 104–108

Study the **Vocabulaire** on page 105.	☐ For additional practice, do Activities 9–10, p. 41 in the **Cahier d'activités.**
	☐ For additional practice, do Activities 5–7, pp. 31–32 in the **Travaux pratiques de grammaire.**
	☐ For additional practice, do Activity 2, CD 1 in the **Interactive CD-ROM Tutor.**
Study the grammar presentation in the **Note de grammaire** box on page 105: reflexive verbs.	☐ Do Activity 18, p. 106 as a writing activity.
	☐ For additional practice, do Activity 3, p. 117 in the **Grammaire supplémentaire.**
Study the expressions in the **Comment dit-on... ?** box on page 106: asking for and making suggestions. You should know how to ask for and give suggestions.	☐ Do Activity 19, p. 107 as a writing activity.
	☐ Do Activity 20, p. 107.
	☐ For additional practice, do Activities 11–13, p. 42 in the **Cahier d'activités.**
Study the expressions in the **Comment dit-on... ?** box on page 107: emphasizing likes and dislikes. You should know how to emphasize what you like and dislike.	☐ For additional practice, do Activity 14, p. 43 in the **Cahier d'activités.**
	☐ For additional practice, do Activity 3, CD 1 in the **Interactive CD-ROM Tutor.**
Study the grammar presentation in the **Note de grammaire** box on page 107: different forms of the reflexive pronoun.	☐ For additional practice, do Activity 8, p. 32 in the **Travaux pratiques de grammaire.**

Study the grammar presentation in the **Note de grammaire** box on page 108: the relative pronouns **ce qui** and **ce que**.

☐ Do Activity 22, p. 108.

☐ Do Activity 23, p. 108 as a writing activity. Write the possible conversation.

☐ Do Activity 24, p. 108.

☐ For additional practice, do Activities 4–6, p. 117 in the **Grammaire supplémentaire**.

☐ For additional practice, do Activities 9–10, p. 33 in the **Travaux pratiques de grammaire**.

■ DEUXIEME ETAPE Self-Test

Can you ask for and make suggestions?	How would you ask what there is to do in Martinique? How would you suggest to your friend to do the activities in the drawings in Activity 4 on the **Que sais-je?** page 122?
Can you emphasize likes and dislikes?	How would you tell someone what you really like to do . . . 1. on Saturday mornings? 2. on weekends? How would you tell someone what you really don't like to do . . . 1. on Sundays? 2. when it's cold? 3. at school?

For an online self-test, go to **go.hrw.com**.

WA3 MARTINIQUE-4

Nom _____ Classe _____ Date _____

4 Sous les tropiques

■ TROISIEME ETAPE Student Make-Up Assignments Checklist

Pupil's Edition, pp. 110–113

Study the **Vocabulaire** on page 111.	☐ For additional practice, do Activities 11–12, p. 34 in the **Travaux pratiques de grammaire**.
Study the expressions in the **Comment dit-on... ?** box on page 111: relating a series of events. You should know how to tell what happened in a sequential order.	☐ Do Activity 27, p. 112 as a writing activity. ☐ For additional practice, do Activities 16–17, p. 44 in the **Cahier d'activités**. ☐ For additional practice, do Activity 4, CD 1 in the **Interactive CD-ROM Tutor**.
Study the grammar presentation in the **Grammaire** box on page 112: the present tense of reflexive verbs.	☐ Do Activity 28, p. 112 as a writing activity. Rewrite the completed sentences. ☐ Do Activity 29, p. 113. ☐ Do Activity 30, p. 113 as a writing activity. ☐ For additional practice, do Activities 7–9, pp. 118–119 in the **Grammaire supplémentaire**. ☐ For additional practice, do Activities 18–21, pp. 45–46 in the **Cahier d'activités**. ☐ For additional practice, do Activities 13–15, pp. 35–36 in the **Travaux pratiques de grammaire**. ☐ For additional practice, do Activity 5, CD 1 in the **Interactive CD-ROM Tutor**.
Study the grammar presentation in the **Note de grammaire** box on page 113: adverbs of frequency.	☐ Do Activity 31, p. 113. ☐ For additional practice, do Activity 10, p. 119 in the **Grammaire supplémentaire**. ☐ For additional practice, do Activity 16, p. 36 in the **Travaux pratiques de grammaire**.

CHAPITRE 4

◼ TROISIEME ETAPE Self-Test

Can you relate a series of events?	How would you tell someone . . . 1. what you do first thing in the morning? 2. what you do after that? 3. what you finally do before leaving for school? Explain what you usually do after school.

 For an online self-test, go to **go.hrw.com**.

WA3 MARTINIQUE-4

Holt French 2 Allez, viens!, Chapter 4

CHAPITRE 5

Quelle journée!

■ PREMIERE ETAPE Student Make-Up Assignments Checklist

Pupil's Edition, pp. 133–137

Study the **Vocabulaire** on page 134.	☐ Do Activity 8, p. 135 as a writing activity. Rewrite the complete sentences.
	☐ For additional practice, do Activities 2–5, pp. 50–51 in the **Cahier d'activités.**
	☐ For additional practice, do Activities 1–4, pp. 37–38 in the **Travaux pratiques de grammaire.**
	☐ For additional practice, do Activity 1, CD 2 in the **Interactive CD-ROM Tutor.**
Study the expressions in the **Comment dit-on... ?** box on page 135: expressing concern for someone. You should know how to express concern for someone.	☐ Do Activity 10, p. 136 as a writing activity.
	☐ Do Activity 11, p. 136 as a writing activity. Write the possible conversation.
	☐ For additional practice, do Activity 7, p. 51 in the **Cahier d'activités.**
Study the grammar presentation in the **Grammaire** box on page 136: the **passé composé.**	☐ Do Activity 13, p. 137.
	☐ Do Activity 14, p. 137.
	☐ Do Activity 16, p. 137 as a writing activity. Write the possible conversations.
	☐ For additional practice, do Activities 1–4, pp. 148–149 in the **Grammaire supplémentaire.**
	☐ For additional practice, do Activities 8–9, p. 52 in the **Cahier d'activités.**
	☐ For additional practice, do Activities 5–8, pp. 39–40 in the **Travaux pratiques de grammaire.**
	☐ For additional practice, do Activity 2, CD 2 in the **Interactive CD-ROM Tutor.**

CHAPITRE 5

■ PREMIERE ETAPE Self-Test

Can you express concern for someone?	How would you show concern for someone by asking what happened?
	How would your friend answer you if the things depicted in Activity 2 of the **Que sais-je?** page 134 happened to him?

For an online self-test, go to **go.hrw.com**.

WA3 TOURAINE-5

CHAPITRE 5

Quelle journée!

■ DEUXIEME ETAPE Student Make-Up Assignments Checklist

Pupil's Edition, pp. 138–141

Study the expressions in the **Comment dit-on... ?** box on page 139: inquiring; expressing satisfaction and frustration. You should know how to ask questions, how to express satisfaction, and how to express frustration.	☐ Do Activity 20, p. 139 as a writing activity. Write the possible conversation. ☐ For additional practice, do Activities 11–12, p. 53 in the **Cahier d'activités.** ☐ For additional practice, do Activities 9–10, p. 41 in the **Travaux pratiques de grammaire.** ☐ For additional practice, do Activity 3, CD 2 in the **Interactive CD-ROM Tutor.**
Study the grammar presentation in the **Grammaire** box on page 140: introduction to the **passé composé** with **être.**	☐ Do Activity 21, p. 140. ☐ Do Activity 22, p. 140. ☐ For additional practice, do Activities 5–9, pp. 149–151 in the **Grammaire supplémentaire.** ☐ For additional practice, do Activities 13–14, pp. 53–54 in the **Cahier d'activités.** ☐ For additional practice, do Activities 11–14, pp. 42–43 in the **Travaux pratiques de grammaire.** ☐ For additional practice, do Activity 4, CD 2 in the **Interactive CD-ROM Tutor.**
Study the expressions in the **Comment dit-on... ?** box on page 141: sympathizing with and consoling someone. You should know how to sympathize and console someone.	☐ Do Activity 24, p. 141 as a writing activity. ☐ Do Activity 25, p. 141. ☐ Do Activity 26, p. 141 as a writing activity. ☐ For additional practice, do Activities 16–17, p. 55 in the **Cahier d'activités.** ☐ For additional practice, do Activity 5, CD 2 in the **Interactive CD-ROM Tutor.**

CHAPITRE 5

■ DEUXIEME ETAPE Self-Test

Can you inquire?	How would you inquire about your friend's . . .
	1. day yesterday?
	2. weekend?
	3. vacation?
Can you express satisfaction and frustration?	How would you respond to someone's question about your weekend if it went really well?
	How would you respond to someone's question about your vacation if everything went wrong?
Can you sympathize with and console someone?	What would you say to sympathize with and console these people?
	1. Céline a raté le bus.
	2. Véronique a été collée.
	3. Henri est arrivé en retard en français.

For an online self-test, go to **go.hrw.com**.

WA3 TOURAINE-5

5 Quelle journée!

CHAPITRE

■ TROISIEME ETAPE Student Make-Up Assignments Checklist

Pupil's Edition, pp. 142–144

Study the expressions in the **Comment dit-on... ?** box on page 143: giving reasons and making excuses. You should know how to give a reason and make excuses.	☐ Do Activity 28, p. 143 as a writing activity. ☐ Do Activity 29, p. 143 as a writing activity. ☐ For additional practice, do Activities 19–21, p. 56 in the **Cahier d'activités.**
Study the expressions in the **Comment dit-on... ?** box on page 143: congratulating and reprimanding someone. You should know how to congratulate or reprimand someone.	☐ Do Activity 31, p. 144 as a writing activity. ☐ Do Activity 32, p. 144 as a writing activity. ☐ Do Activity 33, p. 144 as a writing activity. Write the possible conversation. ☐ Do Activity 34, p. 144 as a writing activity. ☐ For additional practice, do Activity 10, p. 151 in the **Grammaire supplémentaire.** ☐ For additional practice, do Activities 22–23, pp. 57–58 in the **Cahier d'activités.** ☐ For additional practice, do Activities 15–17, p. 44 in the **Travaux pratiques de grammaire.** ☐ For additional practice, do Activity 6, CD 2 in the **Interactive CD-ROM Tutor.**

CHAPITRE 5

■ TROISIEME ETAPE Self-Test

Can you give reasons and make excuses?	How would you explain the grades in the report card in Activity 7 on the **Que sais-je?** page 154?
Can you congratulate and reprimand someone?	What would you say to a friend who . . . 1. got a good grade in French? 2. won an athletic competition? 3. received a scholarship to college? How would you reprimand a friend who . . . 1. got a low grade in English? 2. is always joking in class?

 For an online self-test, go to **go.hrw.com**.

WA3 TOURAINE-5

CHAPITRE 5

CHAPITRE

6 A nous les châteaux!

■ **PREMIERE ETAPE** Student Make-Up Assignments Checklist

Pupil's Edition, pp. 161–165

Study the **Vocabulaire** on page 162.	☐ Do Activity 8, p. 163 as a writing activity. Rewrite the sentences in the order the pictures appear.
	☐ Do Activity 9, p. 163 as a writing activity. Write the possible conversation.
	☐ For additional practice, do Activities 3–4, pp. 62–63 in the **Cahier d'activités**.
	☐ For additional practice, do Activities 1–4, pp. 45–46 in the **Travaux pratiques de grammaire**.
	☐ For additional practice, do Activity 1, CD 2 in the **Interactive CD-ROM Tutor**.
Study the expressions in the **Comment dit-on... ?** box on page 164: asking for opinions; expressing enthusiasm, indifference, and dissatisfaction. You should know how to ask for an opinion, express enthusiasm, indifference, and dissatisfaction.	☐ For additional practice, do Activities 7–8, p. 64 in the **Cahier d'activités**.
	☐ For additional practice, do Activity 2, CD 2 in the **Interactive CD-ROM Tutor**.
Study the grammar presentation in the **Note de grammaire** box on page 164: **c'était**.	☐ Do Activity 11, p. 164 as a writing activity. Rewrite the sentences in the correct order.
	☐ Do Activity 12, p. 165 as a writing activity.
	☐ Do Activity 13, p. 165 as a writing activity.
	☐ Do Activity 15, p. 165 as a writing activity.
	☐ For additional practice, do Activity 3, p. 177 in the **Grammaire supplémentaire**.
	☐ For additional practice, do Activity 5, p. 46 in the **Travaux pratiques de grammaire**.

CHAPITRE 6

■ PREMIERE ETAPE Self-Test

Can you ask for opinions?	How would you ask . . . 1. how your friend's weekend was? 2. if your friend liked what he or she did? 3. if your friend had fun?
Can you express enthusiasm, indifference, and dissatisfaction?	You're just back from a trip, and your friend asks you how it was. How would you respond if you had visisted the places in the pictures in Activity 2 on the **Que sais-je?** Page 183? How would you tell what you did on your last vacation and how you liked it?

For an online self-test, go to **go.hrw.com**.

WA3 TOURAINE-6

CHAPITRE 6

A nous les châteaux!

■ DEUXIEME ETAPE Student Make-Up Assignments Checklist

Pupil's Edition, pp. 166–169

Study the **Vocabulaire** on page 167.	☐ Do Activity 17, p. 167 as a writing activity.
	☐ For additional practice, do Activities 10–11, p. 65 in the **Cahier d'activités.**
	☐ For additional practice, do Activities 6–10, pp. 47–49 in the **Travaux pratiques de grammaire.**
	☐ For additional practice, do Activity 3, CD 2 in the **Interactive CD-ROM Tutor.**
Study the grammar presentation in the **Grammaire** box on page 167: the **passé composé** with **être.**	☐ Do Activity 18, p. 168 as a writing activity.
	☐ Do Activity 19, p. 168 as a writing activity. Write the description.
	☐ For additional practice, do Activities 5 and 8, pp. 177–178 in the **Grammaire supplémentaire.**
	☐ For additional practice, do Activities 12–13, p. 66 in the **Cahier d'activités.**
	☐ For additional practice, do Activities 11–13, pp. 49–50 in the **Travaux pratiques de grammaire.**
	☐ For additional practice, do Activity 4, CD 2 in the **Interactive CD-ROM Tutor.**
Study the expressions in the **Comment dit-on... ?** box on page 168: expressing disbelief and doubt. You should know how to express disbelief and doubt.	☐ Do Activity 21, p. 169. as a writing activity.
	☐ Do Activity 22, p. 169. as a writing activity.
	☐ Do Activity 24, p. 169.
	☐ For additional practice, do Activity 15, p. 67 in the **Cahier d'activités.**

CHAPITRE 6

■ DEUXIEME ETAPE Self-Test

Can you express disbelief and doubt?	How would you respond if your friend told you . . .
	1. she got lost in a dungeon while visiting a castle?
	2. he saw the ghost of Francis I arguing with Leonardo da Vinci?
	3. she found 100 gold coins in the gardens at Chenonceau?
	4. he just inherited the château of Azay-le-Rideau

For an online self-test, go to **go.hrw.com**.

WA3 TOURAINE-6

Holt French 2 Allez, viens!, Chapter 6

CHAPITRE 6

CHAPITRE

6 A nous les châteaux!

■ TROISIEME ETAPE Student Make-Up Assignments Checklist

Pupil's Edition, pp. 171–173

Study the expressions in the **Comment dit-on... ?** box on page 172: asking for and giving information. You should know how to ask for and give information.	☐ For additional practice, do Activities 17–19, pp. 68–69 in the **Cahier d'activités.** ☐ For additional practice, do Activity 5, CD 2 in the **Interactive CD-ROM Tutor.**
Study the grammar presentation in the **Note de grammaire** box on page 172: formal questions.	☐ Do Activity 27, p. 172 as a writing activity. ☐ Do Activity 28, p. 172 as a writing activity. ☐ For additional practice, do Activity 10, p. 179 in the **Grammaire supplémentaire.** ☐ For additional practice, do Activity 20, p. 69 in the **Cahier d'activités.** ☐ For additional practice, do Activities 14–15, p. 51 in the **Travaux pratiques de grammaire.** ☐ For additional practice, do Activity 6, CD 2 in the **Interactive CD-ROM Tutor.**
Study the grammar presentation in the **Note de grammaire** box on page 173: the verb **ouvrir.**	☐ Do Activity 29, p. 173 as a writing activity. ☐ Do Activity 30, p. 173 as a writing activity. Write the possible conversation. ☐ Do Activity 32, p. 173 as a writing activity. ☐ For additional practice, do Activity 11, p. 179 in the **Grammaire supplémentaire.** ☐ For additional practice, do Activity 21, p. 69 in the **Cahier d'activités.** ☐ For additional practice, do Activities 16–17, p. 52 in the **Travaux pratiques de grammaire.**

CHAPITRE 6

■ TROISIEME ETAPE Self-Test

| Can you ask for and give information? | How would you find out . . . |

How would you find out . . .

1. the cost of a round-trip ticket to your destination?
2. which platform the train leaves from?
3. at what time the train leaves?
4. when a place opens and closes?
5. how much it costs to get into a place?

Can you ask someone . . .

1. at what times a museum opens?
2. at what time it closes in the spring?
3. what the regular entrance fee is?
4. what the fee for teenagers is?

Can you give the information above?

For an online self-test, go to **go.hrw.com**.

WA3 TOURAINE-6

7 En pleine forme

■ PREMIERE ETAPE Student Make-Up Assignments Checklist

Pupil's Edition, pp. 189–192

Study the expressions in the **Comment dit-on... ?** box on page 189: expressing concern for someone; complaing. You should know how to express concern for someone and how to say something is wrong.	☐ Do Activity 7, p. 190 as a writing activity. ☐ For additional practice, do Activity 3, p. 74 in the **Cahier d'activités.**
Study the **Vocabulaire** on page 189.	☐ Do Activity 8, p. 190 as a writing activity. Write the possible conversation. ☐ For additional practice, do Activities 4–5, p. 74 in the **Cahier d'activités.** ☐ For additional practice, do Activities 1–2, p. 53 in the **Travaux pratiques de grammaire.**
Study the **Vocabulaire** on page 190.	☐ Do Activity 10, p. 191 as a writing activity. Rewrite the entire sentences. ☐ Do Activity 12, p. 191 as a writing activity. Write the possible conversation. ☐ For additional practice, do Activities 6–7, p. 75 in the **Cahier d'activités.** ☐ For additional practice, do Activities 3–5, pp. 54–55 in the **Travaux pratiques de grammaire.**
Study the **Vocabulaire** on page 191.	☐ Do Activity 14, p. 192 as a writing activity. ☐ Do Activity 15, p. 192. ☐ For additional practice, do Activity 6, p. 55 in the **Travaux pratiques de grammaire.** ☐ For additional practice, do Activity 1, CD 2 in the **Interactive CD-ROM Tutor.**

CHAPITRE 7

Study the grammar presentation in the **Note de grammaire** box on page 192: the **passé composé** of reflexive verbs.

☐ Do Activity 16, p. 192 as a writing activity. Write the possible conversation.

☐ For additional practice, do Activities 2–3, pp. 206–207 in the **Grammaire supplémentaire.**

☐ For additional practice, do Activity 8, p. 76 in the **Cahier d'activités.**

☐ For additional practice, do Activities 7–8, p. 56 in the **Travaux pratiques de grammaire.**

☐ For additional practice, do Activity 2, CD 2 in the **Interactive CD-ROM Tutor.**

■ PREMIERE ETAPE Self-Test

Can you express concern for someone and complain?

What would you say to a friend if . . .

1. he didn't look well?

2. something seemed to be wrong?

3. she were on crutches?

How would you respond to a friend's concern if . . .

1. you were very tired?

2. you weren't feeling well?

3. your arm were in a sling?

4. you had a cold?

5. you'd cut your finger?

6. you'd lifted weights for the first time?

 For an online self-test, go to **go.hrw.com**.

WA3 TOURAINE–7

CHAPITRE **7**

En pleine forme

■ **DEUXIEME ETAPE** Student Make-Up Assignments Checklist

Pupil's Edition, pp. 194–198

Study the **Vocabulaire** on page 195.	☐ Do Activity 20, p. 196 as a writing activity.
	☐ Do Activity 20, p. 196 as a writing activity.
	☐ For additional practice, do Activity 11, p. 77 in the **Cahier d'activités.**
	☐ For additional practice, do Activities 9–11, p. 57 in the **Travaux pratiques de grammaire.**
	☐ For additional practice, do Activity 3, CD 2 in the **Interactive CD-ROM Tutor.**
Study the grammar presentation in the **Note de grammaire** box on page 196: the pronoun **en.**	☐ Do Activity 22, p. 196 as a writing activity.
	☐ For additional practice, do Activities 4–5, pp. 207–208 in the **Grammaire supplémentaire.**
	☐ For additional practice, do Activities 13–14, pp. 58–59 in the **Travaux pratiques de grammaire.**
Study the expressions in the **Comment dit-on... ?** box on page 196: giving advice; accepting, and rejecting advice. You should know how to give, accept, and reject advice.	☐ For additional practice, do Activities 13–14, p. 78 in the **Cahier d'activités.**
Study the grammar presentation in the **Note de grammaire** box on page 197: the verb **devoir.**	☐ Do Activity 24, p. 197.
	☐ Do Activity 25, p. 197 as a writing activity.
	☐ For additional practice, do Activity 6, p. 208 in the **Grammaire supplémentaire.**
	☐ For additional practice, do Activity 15, p. 59 in the **Travaux pratiques de grammaire.**

| Study the expressions in the **Comment dit-on... ?** box on page 198: expressing discouragement and offering encouragement. You should know how to express discouragement and how to offer encouragement. | ☐ Do Activity 28, p. 198.
 ☐ Do Activity 29, p. 198 as a writing activity. Write the possible conversation.
 ☐ For additional practice, do Activities 16–17, p. 79 in the **Cahier d'activités.**
 ☐ For additional practice, do Activity 4, CD 2 in the **Interactive CD-ROM Tutor.** |

■ DEUXIEME ETAPE Self-Test

Can you give advice?	How would you suggest that your friend do the exercises in the pictures in Activity 3 on the **Que sais-je?** page 184?
Can you accept and reject advice?	How would you respond to the suggestions you made in the previous activity?
Can you express discouragement and offer encouragement?	How would you express discouragement if you were . . . 1. on the last mile of a marathon? 2. studying for final exams? 3. in the final minutes of your aerobics class? How would you encourage someone who . . . 1. can't go on? 2. is almost finished? 3. is discouraged about his or her grades?

For an online self-test, go to **go.hrw.com**.

WA3 TOURAINE-7

7 En pleine forme

■ TROISIEME ETAPE Student Make-Up Assignments Checklist

Pupil's Edition, pp. 200–203

Study the **Vocabulaire** on page 201.	☐ Do Activity 31, p. 201 as a writing activity. Write your answers to the questions.
	☐ For additional practice, do Activity 18, p. 80 in the **Cahier d'activités.**
	☐ For additional practice, do Activities 16–17, p. 60 in the **Travaux pratiques de grammaire.**
	☐ For additional practice, do Activity 5, CD 2 in the **Interactive CD-ROM Tutor.**
Study the grammar presentation in the **Note de grammaire** box on page 201: the verb **se nourrir.**	☐ Do Activity 33, p. 202 as a writing activity. Rewrite the paragraph.
	☐ Do Activity 34, p. 202.
	☐ For additional practice, do Activity 8, p. 209 in the **Grammaire supplémentaire.**
	☐ For additional practice, do Activity 21, p. 81 in the **Cahier d'activités.**
	☐ For additional practice, do Activities 18–19, p. 61 in the **Travaux pratiques de grammaire.**
Study the expressions in the **Comment dit-on... ?** box on page 202: justifying your recommendations; advising against something. You should know how to justify what you say and express views against something.	☐ Do Activity 36, p. 203 as a writing activity. Write your advice to them.
	☐ Do Activity 37, p. 203.
	☐ Do Activity 38, p. 203 as a writing activity. Write the possible conversation.
	☐ For additional practice, do Activities 22–23, pp. 81–82 in the **Cahier d'activités.**
	☐ For additional practice, do Activity 6, CD 2 in the **Interactive CD-ROM Tutor.**

CHAPITRE 7

■ TROISIEME ETAPE Self-Test

Can you justify your recommendations and advise against something?	How would tell someone what he or she should do on a regular basis and explain why?
	If a friend were trying to lead a healthy lifestyle, what are three things you would advise him or her to avoid?

For an online self-test, go to **go.hrw.com**.

WA3 TOURAINE-7

CHAPITRE 8

C'était comme ça

■ PREMIÈRE ÉTAPE Student Make-Up Assignments Checklist

Pupil's Edition, pp. 224–227

Study the expressions in the **Comment dit-on... ?** box on page 225: telling what or whom you miss; reassuring someone. You should know how to tell you miss someone or something and how to reassure someone.	☐ Do Activity 8, p. 225 as a writing activity. ☐ Do Activity 9, p. 225. ☐ Do Activity 10, p. 226 as a writing activity. Write the possible conversation. ☐ For additional practice, do Activities 3–5, p. 86 in the **Cahier d'activités.**
Study the expressions in the **Comment dit-on... ?** box on page 226: asking and telling what things were like. You should know how to describe the past.	☐ For additional practice, do Activity 1, p. 240 in the **Grammaire supplémentaire.**
Study the **Vocabulaire** on page 226.	☐ Do Activity 12, p. 227 as a writing activity. ☐ For additional practice, do Activities 6–7, p. 87 in the **Cahier d'activités.** ☐ For additional practice, do Activities 1–4, pp. 62–63 in the **Travaux pratiques de grammaire.** ☐ For additional practice, do Activities 1, CD 2 in the **Interactive CD-ROM Tutor.**
Study the grammar presentation in the **Grammaire** box on page 227: the imperfect of **être** and **avoir.**	☐ Do Activity 13, p. 227 as a writing activity. ☐ Do Activity 14, p. 227. ☐ Do Activity 15, p. 227. ☐ For additional practice, do Activities 2–3, p. 240 in the **Grammaire supplémentaire.** ☐ For additional practice, do Activity 8, p. 88 in the **Cahier d'activités.** ☐ For additional practice, do Activities 5–6, p. 64 in the **Travaux pratiques de grammaire.** ☐ For additional practice, do Activity 2, CD 2 in the **Interactive CD-ROM Tutor.**

CHAPITRE 8

■ PREMIERE ETAPE Self-Test

Can you tell what or whom you miss?	If you moved to a new city, how would you say you missed the things in the pictures in Activity 1 on the **Que sais-je?** page 246?
Can you reassure someone?	How would you reassure someone who had just moved to your town and was homesick?
Can you ask and tell what things were like?	How would you ask your homesick friend what his or her former town was like? How would you describe how things were . . . 1. in medieval times? 2. when you were five?

For an online self-test, go to **go.hrw.com**.

WA3 COTE D'IVOIRE-8

CHAPITRE 8

CHAPITRE 8

C'était comme ça

■ DEUXIEME ETAPE Student Make-Up Assignments Checklist

Pupil's Edition, pp. 228–232

Study the **Vocabulaire** on page 228.	☐ Do Activity 16, p. 229 as a writing activity.
	☐ For additional practice, do Activities 10–11, p. 89 in the **Cahier d'activités.**
	☐ For additional practice, do Activities 7–10, pp. 65–66 in the **Travaux pratiques de grammaire.**
Study the expressions in the **Comment dit-on... ?** box on page 229: reminiscing. You should know how to talk about the past.	☐ Do Activity 18, p. 229 as a writing activity.
	☐ For additional practice, do Activity 3, CD 2 in the **Interactive CD-ROM Tutor.**
Study the grammar presentation in the **Grammaire** box on page 230: the imperfect.	☐ Do Activity 20, p. 230.
	☐ Do Activity 21, p. 231 as a writing activity.
	☐ Do Activity 22, p. 231 as a writing activity. Write the answers to your questions.
	☐ Do Activity 23, p. 232 as a writing activity.
	☐ Do Activity 25, p. 232.
	☐ For additional practice, do Activities 4–7, pp. 241–242 in the **Grammaire supplémentaire.**
	☐ For additional practice, do Activities 13–15, pp. 90–91 in the **Cahier d'activités.**
	☐ For additional practice, do Activities 11–15, pp. 67–68 in the **Travaux pratiques de grammaire.**
	☐ For additional practice, do Activity 4, CD 2 in the **Interactive CD-ROM Tutor.**

CHAPITRE 8

Holt French 2 Allez, viens!, Chapter 8

■ DEUXIEME ETAPE Self-Test

Can you reminisce?	How would you tell what these people used to do when they were young? Look at the drawings in Activity 5 on the **Que sais-je?** page 246?
	How would you tell what you usually did after school when you were ten years old?

 For an online self-test, go to **go.hrw.com**.

WA3 COTE D'IVOIRE-8

CHAPITRE 8

CHAPITRE 8

C'était comme ça

■ TROISIEME ETAPE Student Make-Up Assignments Checklist

Pupil's Edition, pp. 234–237

Study the **Vocabulaire** on page 236.	☐ Do Activity 28, p. 236.
	☐ Do Activity 29, p. 237.
	☐ For additional practice, do Activities 16–18, pp. 92–93 in the **Cahier d'activités.**
	☐ For additional practice, do Activities 16–17, p. 69 in the **Travaux pratiques de grammaire.**
	☐ For additional practice, do Activities 5–6, CD 2 in the **Interactive CD-ROM Tutor.**
Study the expressions in the **Comment dit-on... ?** box on page 237: making and responding to suggestions. You should know how to make and respond to suggestions.	☐ Do Activity 30, p. 237 as a writing activity.
	☐ For additional practice, do Activities 19–21, pp. 93–94 in the **Cahier d'activités.**
Study the grammar presentation in the **Note de grammaire** box on page 237: how to make suggestions with the imperfect.	☐ Do Activity 31, p. 237 as a writing activity.
	☐ Do Activity 32, p. 237 as a writing activity. Write the possible conversation.
	☐ For additional practice, do Activity 8–10, p. 243 in the **Grammaire supplémentaire.**
	☐ For additional practice, do Activity 18–19, p. 70 in the **Travaux pratiques de grammaire.**

CHAPITRE 8

■ TROISIEME ETAPE Self-Test

Can you make and respond to suggestions?	How would you suggest . . .
	1. visiting a place in Abidjan?
	2. buying something from the market?
	3. playing your favorite game or sport?
	How would you respond if a friend invited you to . . .
	1. play tennis?
	2. eat barbecue?
	3. visit a museum?

 For an online self-test, go to **go.hrw.com**.

WA3 COTE D'IVOIRE-8

CHAPITRE 8

Tu connais la nouvelle?

■ PREMIERE ETAPE Student Make-Up Assignments Checklist

Pupil's Edition, pp. 257–260

Study the **Vocabulaire** on page 258.	☐ Do Activity 8, p. 258.
	☐ Do Activity 9, p. 258.
	☐ For additional practice, do Activities 3–5, p. 98 in the **Cahier d'activités**.
	☐ For additional practice, do Activities 1–3, pp. 71–72 in the **Travaux pratiques de grammaire**.
	☐ For additional practice, do Activity 1, CD 3 in the **Interactive CD-ROM Tutor**.
Study the grammar presentation in the **Note de grammaire** box on page 259: the imperfect and the expression **avoir l'air**.	☐ Do Activity 10, p. 259.
	☐ For additional practice, do Activities 1–3, pp. 272–273 in the **Grammaire supplémentaire**.
	☐ For additional practice, do Activities 4–5, p. 72 in the **Travaux pratiques de grammaire**.
Study the expressions in the **Comment dit-on... ?** box on page 260: wondering what happened; offering possible explanations; accepting or rejecting explanations. You should know how to consider what happened, offer, accept, and reject possible explanations.	☐ Do Activity 12, p. 260 as a writing activity. Write the possible conversations.
	☐ Do Activity 13, p. 260.
	☐ For additional practice, do Activities 6–8, pp. 99–100 in the **Cahier d'activités**.
	☐ For additional practice, do Activity 2, CD 3 in the **Interactive CD-ROM Tutor**.

■ PREMIERE ETAPE Self-Test

Can you wonder what happened and offer possible explanations?	If you didn't know why your friend was late for your meeting after school, how would you say that you wonder what happened?
	What possible explanations could you give for each of these situations?
	1. Ton ami(e) était déprimé(e).
	2. Tes parents avaient l'air fâchés aujourd'hui.
	3. Ton prof était de bonne humeur.
	4. Tes amis étaient étonnés.
Can you accept and reject explanations?	How would you respond if your friends made these remarks?
	1. «A mon avis, il va faire beau aujourd'hui.»
	2. «Je crois que Paris est la plus grande ville de France.»
	3. «Je parie que j'ai raté mon interro d'anglais.»
	4. «Peut-être que notre prof est en retard.»
	5. «J'ai vu un extraterrestre dans le jardin.»

 For an online self-test, go to **go.hrw.com**.

WA3 PROVENCE-9

Holt French 2 Allez, viens!, Chapter 9

CHAPITRE 9

CHAPITRE

9 Tu connais la nouvelle?

■ DEUXIEME ETAPE Student Make-Up Assignments Checklist

Pupil's Edition, pp. 262–266

Study the **Vocabulaire** on page 263.	☐ Do Activity 16, p. 263.
	☐ For additional practice, do Activities 10–12, pp. 101–102 in the **Cahier d'activités.**
	☐ For additional practice, do Activities 6–7, p. 73 in the **Travaux pratiques de grammaire.**
	☐ For additional practice, do Activity 3, CD 3 in the **Interactive CD-ROM Tutor.**
Study the expressions in the **Comment dit-on... ?** box on page 263: breaking some news; showing interest. You should know how to give news to someone and how to show interest.	☐ Do Activity 18, p. 264 as a writing activity.
	☐ For additional practice, do Activity 13, p. 102 in the **Cahier d'activités.**
Study the grammar presentation in the **Grammaire** box on page 265: the **passé composé** versus the **imparfait.**	☐ Do Activity 19, p. 265 as a writing activity. Rewrite the each verb and next to it the tense.
	☐ Do Activity 20, p. 266 as a writing activity.
	☐ Do Activity 21, p. 266 as a writing activity.
	☐ Do Activity 22, p. 266.
	☐ For additional practice, do Activities 4–7, p. 274–275 in the **Grammaire supplémentaire.**
	☐ For additional practice, do Activity 14, p. 103 in the **Cahier d'activités.**
	☐ For additional practice, do Activities 8–12, pp. 74–76 in the **Travaux pratiques de grammaire.**
	☐ For additional practice, do Activity 4, CD 3 in the **Interactive CD-ROM Tutor.**

CHAPITRE 9

■ DEUXIEME ETAPE Self-Test

Can you break some news?	If you break the news represented in the drawings in Activity 4 on the **Que sais-je?** page 242?
Can you show interest?	How would you respond if your friend said **Devine ce qui s'est passé hier?**

 For an online self-test, go to **go.hrw.com**.

WA3 PROVENCE-9

CHAPITRE 9

CHAPITRE 9

Tu connais la nouvelle?

■ TROISIEME ETAPE Student Make-Up Assignments Checklist

Pupil's Edition, pp. 267–269

Study the expressions in the **Comment dit-on... ?** box on page 267: beginning, continuing, and ending a story. You should know how to begin, continue, and end a story.	☐ Do Activity 25, p. 268. ☐ For additional practice, do Activities 16–17, p. 104 in the **Cahier d'activités.** ☐ For additional practice, do Activity 5, CD 3 in the **Interactive CD-ROM Tutor.**
Study the grammar presentation in the **Note de grammaire** box on page 269: more of the **passé composé** versus the **imparfait,** and the usage of the phrase **en train de.**	☐ Do Activity 27, p. 269. ☐ Do Activity 28, p. 269. ☐ For additional practice, do Activities 8–9, p. 275 in the **Grammaire supplémentaire.** ☐ For additional practice, do Activities 18–20, pp. 105–106 in the **Cahier d'activités.** ☐ For additional practice, do Activities 13–14, p. 77 in the **Travaux pratiques de grammaire.** ☐ For additional practice, do Activity 6, CD 3 in the **Interactive CD-ROM Tutor.**

CHAPITRE 9

■ TROISIEME ETAPE Self-Test

Can you begin, continue, and end a story?	What would you say to begin a story you'd like to tell?
	What would you say to continue the story you began in the previous activity?
	What would you say if your story ended well? If it ended badly?

For an online self-test, go to **go.hrw.com**.

WA3 PROVENCE-9

Holt French 2 Allez, viens!, Chapter 10

CHAPITRE 9

10 Je peux te parler?

■ PREMIERE ETAPE Student Make-Up Assignments Checklist

Pupil's Edition, pp. 285–289

Study the expressions in the **Comment dit-on... ?** box on page 286: sharing a confidence. You should know how to share confidences.	☐ For additional practice, do Activity 3, p. 110 in the **Cahier d'activités.**
Study the expressions in the **Comment dit-on... ?** box on page 286: asking for and giving advice. You should know how to ask for and give advice.	☐ Do Activity 8, p.287 as a writing activity. Rewrite the answers in the right order. ☐ For additional practice, do Activities 4–5, pp. 110–111 in the **Cahier d'activités.** ☐ For additional practice, do Activity 1, CD 3 in the **Interactive CD-ROM Tutor.**
Study the **Vocabulaire** on page 287.	☐ For additional practice, do Activities 1–4, pp. 78–80 in the **Travaux pratiques de grammaire.** ☐ For additional practice, do Activity 2, CD 3 in the **Interactive CD-ROM Tutor.**
Study the grammar presentation in the **Grammaire** box on page 288: object pronouns and their placement.	☐ Do Activity 12, p. 289. ☐ Do Activity 13, p. 289 as a writing activity. ☐ Do Activity 14, p. 289 as a writing activity. Write the possible conversation. ☐ For additional practice, do Activity 1-6, pp. 300-301 in the **Grammaire supplémentaire.** ☐ For additional practice, do Activity 8, p. 112 in the **Cahier d'activités.** ☐ For additional practice, do Activities 5–7, pp. 80–81 in the **Travaux pratiques de grammaire.** ☐ For additional practice, do Activity 3, CD 3 in the **Interactive CD-ROM Tutor.**

CHAPITRE 10

■ PREMIERE ETAPE Self-Test

Can you share a confidence?	How would you approach your friend if you had a problem?
	How would you respond if a friend approached you with a problem?
Can you ask for and give advice?	How would you ask a friend for advice about doing better in one of your classes?
	How would you advise your friend to . . . 1. apologize? 2. forgive her boyfriend? 3. telephone his parents?

For an online self-test, go to **go.hrw.com**.

WA3 PROVENCE-10

10 Je peux te parler?

■ DEUXIEME ETAPE Student Make-Up Assignments Checklist

Pupil's Edition, pp. 290–293

Study the expressions in the **Comment dit-on... ?** box on page 291: asking for and granting a favor; making excuses. You should know how to ask for a favor and how to make excuses.	☐ Do Activity 17, p. 291. ☐ For additional practice, do Activity 11, p. 114 in the **Cahier d'activités**.
Study the **Vocabulaire** on page 291.	☐ Do Activity 19, p. 292 as a writing activity. ☐ Do Activity 20, p. 292 as a writing activity. ☐ For additional practice, do Activity 12, p. 114 in the **Cahier d'activités**. ☐ For additional practice, do Activities 8–10, pp. 82–83 in the **Travaux pratiques de grammaire**. ☐ For additional practice, do Activity 4, CD 3 in the **Interactive CD-ROM Tutor**.
Study the grammar presentation in the **Note de grammaire** box on page 293: the **passé composé** and the direct object pronouns.	☐ Do Activity 22, p. 293. ☐ Do Activity 23, p. 293 as a writing activity. Write the possible skit. ☐ For additional practice, do Activities 7-10, pp. 302-303 in the **Grammaire supplémentaire**. ☐ For additional practice, do Activities 14–15, p. 115 in the **Cahier d'activités**. ☐ For additional practice, do Activities 11–14, pp. 84–85 in the **Travaux pratiques de grammaire**. ☐ For additional practice, do Activity 5, CD 3 in the **Interactive CD-ROM Tutor**.

CHAPITRE 10

■ DEUXIEME ETAPE Self-Test

Can you ask for a favor?	How would you ask a friend to do the things in the pictures in Activity 5 on the **Que sais-je?** page 306?
Can you grant a favor and make excuses?	How would you respond if your friend asked you for the following favors? 1. «Ça t'embête de téléphoner à Catherine?» 2. «Tu pourrais sortir la poubelle, s'il te plaît?» 3. «Ça t'ennuie de me prêter 200 euros?»

For an online self-test, go to **go.hrw.com**.

WA3 PROVENCE-10

CHAPITRE 10

Je peux te parler?

■ TROISIEME ETAPE Student Make-Up Assignments Checklist

Pupil's Edition, pp. 294–296

Study the expressions in the **Comment dit-on... ?** box on page 294: apologizing and accepting an apology; reproaching someone. You should know how to ask for an apology, how to accept an apology, and how to reproach someone.	☐ Do Activity 26, p. 295 as a writing activity. ☐ Do Activity 27, p. 295 as a writing activity. ☐ For additional practice, do Activities 16–18, pp. 116–117 in the **Cahier d'activités.** ☐ For additional practice, do Activity 6, CD 3 in the **Interactive CD-ROM Tutor.**
Study the grammar presentation in the **Note de grammaire** box on page 295: the use of infinitive and object pronouns.	☐ Do Activity 28, p. 296. ☐ Do Activity 29, p. 296 as a writing activity. Write the possible scene. ☐ Do Activity 30, p. 296. ☐ Do Activity 31, p. 296. ☐ For additional practice, do Activities 11-12, p. 303 in the **Grammaire supplémentaire.** ☐ For additional practice, do Activity 19, p. 117 in the **Cahier d'activités.** ☐ For additional practice, do Activities 15–16, p. 86 in the **Travaux pratiques de grammaire.**

Nom _____ Classe _____ Date _____

■ TROISIEME ETAPE Self-Test

Can you apologize and accept an apology?	How would you apologize to a friend with whom you had a misunderstanding? How would you respond if your friend said . . . 1. «J'ai perdu ton livre. C'est de ma faute.» 2. «Je suis désolé(e) de ne pas être venu(e) à ta fête hier soir.» 3. «Tu ne m'en veux pas?»
Can you reproach someone?	How would you reproach a friend who was late meeting you at the movies?

 For an online self-test, go to **go.hrw.com**.

WA3 PROVENCE-10

CHAPITRE 11 Chacun ses goûts

■ PREMIERE ETAPE Student Make-Up Assignments Checklist

Pupil's Edition, pp. 313–317

Study the expressions in the **Comment dit-on... ?** box on page 313: identifying people and things. You should know how to identify people and things.	☐ For additional practice, do Activity 2, p. 122 in the **Cahier d'activités.**
Study the grammar presentation in the **Note de grammaire** box on page 314: the verb **connaître.**	☐ Do Activity 8, p. 314 as a writing activity. ☐ For additional practice, do Activity 1, p. 330 in the **Grammaire supplémentaire.** ☐ For additional practice, do Activity 3, p. 122 in the **Cahier d'activités.** ☐ For additional practice, do Activities 1–2, pp. 87–88 in the **Travaux pratiques de grammaire.**
Study the **Vocabulaire** on page 314.	☐ Do Activity 9, p. 315 as a writing activity. ☐ Do Activity 10, p. 315 as a writing activity. ☐ For additional practice, do Activity 4, p. 123 in the **Cahier d'activités.** ☐ For additional practice, do Activities 3–4, p. 88 in the **Travaux pratiques de grammaire.**
Study the grammar presentation in the **Note de grammaire** box on page 315: **il/elle est...** versus **c'est...**	☐ Do Activity 11, p. 315 as a writing activity. ☐ For additional practice, do Activities 2-4, pp. 330-331 in the **Grammaire supplémentaire.** ☐ For additional practice, do Activity 6, p. 123 in the **Cahier d'activités.** ☐ For additional practice, do Activities 5–7, p. 89 in the **Travaux pratiques de grammaire.** ☐ For additional practice, do Activity 1, CD 3 in the **Interactive CD-ROM Tutor.**

CHAPITRE 11

Study the **Vocabulaire** on page 316.	☐ Do Activity 13, p. 316 as a writing activity.
	☐ Do Activity 16, p. 316.
	☐ Do Activity 17, p. 316 as a writing activity. Write what you would do and who would be the stars in your **Fête de la musique**.
	☐ For additional practice, do Activities 7–8, p. 124 in the **Cahier d'activités**.
	☐ For additional practice, do Activities 8–11, pp. 90–91 in the **Travaux pratiques de grammaire**.
	☐ For additional practice, do Activity 2, CD 3 in the **Interactive CD-ROM Tutor**.

■ PREMIERE ETAPE Self-Test

Can you identify people and things?	How would you ask a friend if she's familiar with your favorite singer? If she isn't, how would you identify the person?
	How would you respond if someone asked you if you were familiar with . . .
	1. *La vie en rose?*
	2. Céline Dion?
	3. Patrick Bruel?
	4. Kassav'?

 For an online self-test, go to **go.hrw.com**.

WA3 PROVENCE-11

CHAPITRE 11
Chacun ses goûts

■ DEUXIEME ETAPE Student Make-Up Assignments Checklist

Pupil's Edition, pp. 319–322

Study the expressions in the **Comment dit-on... ?** box on page 320: asking for and giving information. You should know how to ask for and give information.	☐ Do Activity 20, p. 320 as a writing activity. ☐ Do Activity 21, p. 320 as a writing activity. Write the possible conversation. ☐ For additional practice, do Activities 10–11, pp. 125–126 in the **Cahier d'activités.** ☐ For additional practice, do Activity 3, CD 3 in the **Interactive CD-ROM Tutor.**
Study the **Vocabulaire** on page 321.	☐ Do Activity 23, p. 322. ☐ Do Activity 24, p. 322 as a writing activity. ☐ Do Activity 25, p. 322 as a writing activity. ☐ Do Activity 26, p. 322 as a writing activity. Write the possible conversation. ☐ Do Activity 27, p. 322. ☐ For additional practice, do Activities 12–13, pp. 126–127 in the **Cahier d'activités.** ☐ For additional practice, do Activities 12–15, pp. 92–93 in the **Travaux pratiques de grammaire.**

CHAPITRE 11

■ DEUXIEME ETAPE Self-Test

Can you ask for and give information?	How would you ask a friend . . .
	1. what movies are playing?
	2. where a movie is playing?
	3. who stars in a movie?
	4. what time something starts?
	According to the movie listing in Activity 4 on the **Que sais-je?** page 336, how would you tell a friend what is playing tonight, where, and at what time?

For an online self-test, go to **go.hrw.com**.

WA3 PROVENCE-11

Holt French 2 Allez, viens!, Chapter 11

CHAPITRE 11

CHAPITRE 11

Chacun ses goûts

■ TROISIEME ETAPE Student Make-Up Assignments Checklist

Pupil's Edition, pp. 324–327

Study the expressions in the **Comment dit-on... ?** box on page 324: giving opinions. You should know how to give your opinion.	☐ Do Activity 30, p. 325. ☐ For additional practice, do Activity 15, p. 128 in the **Cahier d'activités.**
Study the **Vocabulaire** on page 325.	☐ Do Activity 32, p. 325 as a writing activity. Write the possible conversation. ☐ For additional practice, do Activity 16, p. 128 in the **Cahier d'activités.** ☐ For additional practice, do Activities 16–18, pp. 94–95 in the **Travaux pratiques de grammaire.** ☐ For additional practice, do Activity 4, CD 3 in the **Interactive CD-ROM Tutor.**
Study the expressions in the **Comment dit-on... ?** box on page 326: summarizing. You should know how to summarize.	☐ Do Activity 33, p. 326 as a writing activity. Rewrite the sentences and place the title of the film next to it. ☐ For additional practice, do Activity 20, p. 129 in the **Cahier d'activités.** ☐ For additional practice, do Activity 5, CD 3 in the **Interactive CD-ROM Tutor.**
Study the grammar presentation in the **Grammaire** box on page 327: the relative pronouns **qui** and **que.**	☐ Do Activity 34, p. 327 as a writing activity. ☐ Do Activity 35, p. 327 as a writing activity. ☐ Do Activity 37, p. 327. ☐ For additional practice, do Activities 5-7 pp. 332-333 in the **Grammaire supplémentaire.** ☐ For additional practice, do Activities 21–22, p. 130 in the **Cahier d'activités.** ☐ For additional practice, do Activities 19–21, pp. 96–97 in the **Travaux pratiques de grammaire.** ☐ For additional practice, do Activity 6, CD 3 in the **Interactive CD-ROM Tutor.**

■ TROISIEME ETAPE Self-Test

Can you give opinions?	What's your opinion of . . .
	1. the play *Romeo and Juliet?*
	2. romance novels?
	3. westerns?
	4. *To Kill a Mockingbird?*
	5. classical music?
	6. *La Cantatrice chauve?*
	What would you say about the last book you read that you liked? The last movie you saw that you didn't like?
Can you summarize?	How would you summarize the plot of . . .
	1. your favorite film?
	2. your favorite book?

 For an online self-test, go to **go.hrw.com**.

WA3 PROVENCE-11

CHAPITRE 11

CHAPITRE

12 A la belle étoile

■ PREMIERE ETAPE Student Make-Up Assignments Checklist

Pupil's Edition, pp. 347–351

Study the expressions in the **Comment dit-on... ?** box on page 348: asking for and giving information; giving directions. You should know how to ask for and give directions.	☐ Do Activity 8, p. 348 as a writing activity. Write the possible conversation. ☐ Do Activity 9, p. 349 as a writing activity. ☐ For additional practice, do Activities 2–4, pp. 134–135 in the **Cahier d'activités.** ☐ For additional practice, do Activity 1, CD 3 in the **Interactive CD-ROM Tutor.**
Study the **Vocabulaire** on page 349.	☐ Do Activity 11, p. 350 as a writing activity. ☐ Do Activity 12, p. 350 as a writing activity. ☐ For additional practice, do Activity 5, p. 135 in the **Cahier d'activités.** ☐ For additional practice, do Activities 1–3, p. 98 in the **Travaux pratiques de grammaire.** ☐ For additional practice, do Activity 2, CD 3 in the **Interactive CD-ROM Tutor.**
Study the **Vocabulaire** on page 350.	☐ Do Activity 13, p. 351 as a writing activity. Rewrite the sentence and your answer next to it. ☐ Do Activity 15, p. 351 as a writing activity. ☐ Do Activity 16, p. 351. ☐ Do Activity 17, p. 351 as a writing activity. ☐ For additional practice, do Activity 6, p. 136 in the **Cahier d'activités.** ☐ For additional practice, do Activities 4–6, p. 99 in the **Travaux pratiques de grammaire.**

CHAPITRE 12

■ PREMIERE ETAPE Self-Test

Can you ask for and give information?	How would you ask someone what there is to see and do in these places? How would you tell someone what there is to see and to do in these places?
	1. in a Canadian park
	2. in Abidjan
	3. in your favorite city
Can you give directions?	How would you ask where these places are? How would you tell where they are?
	1. le parc de la Jacques-Cartier
	2. la Côte d'Ivoire
	3. la Martinique

 For an online self-test, go to **go.hrw.com**.

WA3 QUEBEC-12

CHAPITRE 12

A la belle étoile

■ DEUXIEME ETAPE Student Make-Up Assignments Checklist

Pupil's Edition, pp. 352–356

Study the **Vocabulaire** on page 353.	☐ Do Activity 19, p. 353 as a writing activity. ☐ Do Activity 20, p. 354. ☐ For additional practice, do Activities 8–9, p. 137 in the **Cahier d'activités**. ☐ For additional practice, do Activities 7–8, pp. 100–101 in the **Travaux pratiques de grammaire**. ☐ For additional practice, do Activity 3, CD 3 in the **Interactive CD-ROM Tutor**.
Study the grammar presentation in the **Note de grammaire** box on page 354: the verb **emporter**.	☐ For additional practice, do Activities 4-5, pp. 365-366 in the **Grammaire supplémentaire**. ☐ For additional practice, do Activities 10–11, p. 102 in the **Travaux pratiques de grammaire**.
Study the expressions in the **Comment dit-on... ?** box on page 354: complaining; expressing discouragement and offering encouragement. You should know how to say what is wrong, how to express discouragement, and how to offer encouragement.	☐ Do Activity 21, p. 354 as a writing activity. ☐ Do Activity 22, p. 354 as a writing activity. Write the possible scene. ☐ For additional practice, do Activity 11, p. 138 in the **Cahier d'activités**. ☐ For additional practice, do Activity 4, CD 3 in the **Interactive CD-ROM Tutor**.
Study the **Vocabulaire** on page 355.	☐ Do Activity 23, p. 355 as a writing activity. ☐ For additional practice, do Activity 12, p. 139 in the **Cahier d'activités**. ☐ For additional practice, do Activities 12–14, p. 103 in the **Travaux pratiques de grammaire**.
Study the expressions in the **Comment dit-on... ?** box on page 356: asking for and giving advice. You should know how to ask for and give advice.	☐ Do Activity 25, p. 356 as a writing activity. ☐ Do Activity 26, p. 356. ☐ Do Activity 27, p. 356. ☐ For additional practice, do Activity 13, p. 139 in the **Cahier d'activités**.

CHAPITRE 12

■ DEUXIEME ETAPE Self-Test

Can you complain and express discouragement?	What would you say if . . . 1. you were on a hike and just couldn't go on? 2. you hadn't eaten since 5:00 this morning? 3. you were afraid of a certain animal?
Can you offer encouragement?	How would you encourage your friend to finish the hike?
Can you ask for and give advice?	How would you ask someone for advice? What would you advise a friend to pack for a camping trip . . . 1. in the summer? 2. in the winter? What advice would you give a friend who . . . 1. is being bitten by mosquitos? 2. is offering some potato chips to a squirrel? 3. just threw the potato chip bag on the ground?

 For an online self-test, go to **go.hrw.com**.

WA3 QUEBEC-12

CHAPITRE 12

CHAPITRE 12

A la belle étoile

■ **TROISIEME ETAPE** Student Make-Up Assignments Checklist

Pupil's Edition, pp. 358–360

Study the expressions in the **Comment dit-on... ?** box on page 358: relating a series of events; describing people and places. You should know how to talk about a series of events in order and how to describe people and places.	☐ For additional practice, do Activities 15–16, p. 140 in the **Cahier d'activités.** ☐ For additional practice, do Activity 5, CD 3 in the **Interactive CD-ROM Tutor.**
Study the grammar presentation in the **Grammaire** box on page 359: the **passé composé** and the **imparfait.**	☐ Do Activity 30, p. 359 as a writing activity. ☐ Do Activity 31, p. 360 as a writing activity. ☐ Do Activity 32, p. 360. ☐ Do Activity 33, p. 360 as a writing activity. Write the possible conversation. ☐ For additional practice, do Activity 6-9, pp. 366-367 in the **Grammaire supplémentaire.** ☐ For additional practice, do Activities 17–19, pp. 140–142 in the **Cahier d'activités.** ☐ For additional practice, do Activities 15–20, pp. 104–107 in the **Travaux pratiques de grammaire.** ☐ For additional practice, do Activity 6, CD 3 in the **Interactive CD-ROM Tutor.**

CHAPITRE 12

■ TROISIEME ETAPE Self-Test

Can you relate a series of events and describe people and places?	How would you say that you did the activities in the drawings in Activity 8 on the **Que sais-je?** page 370 in the order in which the drawings appear?
	How would you describe . . .
	1. the weather yesterday?
	2. how you felt this morning?

For an online self-test, go to **go.hrw.com**.

WA3 QUEBEC-12

Alternative Quizzes

Bon séjour!

Alternative Quiz 1-1A

Maximum Score: 30/100

■ PREMIERE ETAPE

Grammar and Vocabulary

A. Alexandre and Blandine are twins. Write a description of Blandine based on these descriptions of Alexandre. (4 points)

1. Alexandre est gourmand. _____

2. Alexandre est jeune. _____

3. Alexandre est brun. _____

4. Alexandre est petit. _____

SCORE [   ]

B. Write a sentence describing each of the following people or characters. Mention one trait each one has and one trait each one doesn't have. (12 points)

1. Kermit the frog®

_____

_____

2. Pete Sampras _____

_____

3. le président des Etats-Unis

_____

_____

4. Céline Dion _____

_____

5. Je _____

_____

6. Mon ami(e) _____

_____

SCORE [   ]

Alternative Quiz 1-1A

CHAPITRE 1

C. Fill in the blanks with the appropriate present tense form of the verb in parentheses. (6 points)

1. Nous _____ (*regarder*) la télé.

2. Tu _____ (*écouter*) de la musique française?

3. Ils _____ (*adorer*) faire de l'équitation.

4. Je _____ (*marcher*) sur la plage.

5. Vous _____ (*acheter*) des CDs?

6. Il _____ (*manger*) au restaurant.

SCORE [   ]

D. Albert is writing to Adèle about his family. Complete his letter with the appropriate form of the verbs **avoir** or **être**. (4 points)

Salut Adèle,

Comment ça va? Voici quelques photos de ma famille. Mes sœurs Agnès et Aurélie **(1)** _____ les cheveux blonds, mais moi, je/j' **(2)** _____ brun. Je/J'

(3) _____ les yeux verts. Mes parents

(4) _____ assez jeunes. Mon père

(5) _____ 50 ans et il est professeur à l'université ici. Ma mère **(6)** _____ blonde, intelligente et super sympa! Comme tu vois, nous

(7) _____ tous un peu gros. Nous adorons manger! Et toi, tu **(8)** _____ comment?

Ecris-moi vite!
Albert

SCORE [   ]

TOTAL SCORE [   ] /30

CHAPITRE 1

Bon séjour!

DEUXIEME ETAPE

Alternative Quiz 1-2A

Maximum Score: 40/100

Grammar and Vocabulary

A. Your friends are about to go on a trip and you're giving them advice on what to do. Use commands to tell them what to do or not do. (10 points)

1. (Claudine) aller acheter / un appareil-photo

_____

2. (Christine et Bernard) ne pas oublier / ton passeport

_____

3. (Cédric) penser à prendre / photos / pendant ton voyage

_____

4. (Corinne et Danielle) ne pas parler / anglais / en France

_____

5. (Delphine) acheter /cartes postales

_____

SCORE _____

B. Denis is going on a trip. Help him decide what to do to get ready. Match each situation with the advice you would give Denis. (10 points)

_____ 1. Je vais sortir le soir.

_____ 2. Je vais prendre des photos.

_____ 3. Il fait un peu froid.

_____ 4. Je vais aller au Québec.

_____ 5. Je ne parle pas très bien français.

a. N'oublie pas ton dictionnaire.

b. Prends ton appareil-photo.

c. Pense à prendre ton passeport.

d. Mets une belle chemise.

e. Prends ton anorak.

SCORE _____

Alternative Quiz 1-2A

C. Based on what each person is doing, choose what he or she is <u>not</u> going to wear. (10 points)

1. Céline va jouer au tennis.

   a. un maillot de bain   **b.** un short   **c.** des baskets

2. Christelle va au théâtre avec sa famille.

   a. un maillot de bain   **b.** une jupe noire   **c.** une chemise blanche

3. Antoine va dîner dans un restaurant chic.

   a. des baskets   **b.** une chemise   **c.** une cravate

4. Tu vas à ton cours d'espagnol.

   a. un jean   **b.** un maillot de bain **c.** un tee-shirt

5. Je vais à la piscine.

   a. un maillot de bain   **b.** un manteau   **c.** des lunettes de soleil

SCORE [   ]

D. Solve these riddles with the appropriate word or phrase in French. (10 points)

1. You need this to bord the plane.

   _____

2. This will keep you warm when you ski.

   _____

3. You need to wear this around your neck when it's cold.

   _____

4. You use this when it rains.

   _____

5. You wear these on your feet when you play tennis.

   _____

SCORE [   ]

TOTAL SCORE [   ] **/40**

Nom_____ Classe_____ Date_____

CHAPITRE 1

1 Bon séjour!

■ TROISIEME ETAPE

Maximum Score: 30/100

Grammar and Vocabulary

A. Based on what the following people like, tell where they're going to go or what they're going to do next weekend. Use the verb **aller** in each of your answers. (10 points)

1. Hélène aime nager.

_____

2. Moi, j'aime l'art.

_____

3. Christophe et Daniel aiment les films.

_____

4. Vous adorez la cuisine vietnamienne.

_____

5. David et moi, nous aimons la campagne.

_____

SCORE ☐

B. You're telling your friends what you plan to do on Saturday. Put the following list of activities in the correct order by numbering them from 1 to 4. (4 points)

_____ Puis, après le déjeuner, je vais acheter des cartes postales pour un ami.

_____ Finalement, je vais aller au parc avec Christian.

_____ D'abord, je vais au Louvre.

_____ Ensuite, je vais retrouver des amis au café vers midi.

SCORE ☐

CHAPITRE 1

Alternative Quiz 1-3A

C. Dominique and her friends are trying to decide what to do after school. Complete their conversations with words and phrases from the box below. (6 points)

> idée   bien   question   envie   pourrait
>
> d'accord   Ça ne me dit   Ça te dit

1. — Qu'est-ce qu'on fait?

   — _____ de jouer au foot?

   — C'est une bonne _____ .

2. — Tu as _____ de faire les magasins avec moi?

   — _____ rien.

3. — Qu'est-ce qu'on fait cet après-midi?

   — On _____ aller au cinéma.

   — Pas _____ ! J'ai trop de devoirs.

SCORE _____

D. You're at the train station. Using official time, write a complete sentence telling when each of these trains arrives. (10 points)

1. Le train de Lille / 11:15 A.M.

   _____

2. Le train de Biarritz / 10:30 P.M.

   _____

3. Le train de Toulouse / 4:45 P.M.

   _____

4. Le train de Poitiers / 7:20 P.M.

   _____

5. Le train de Dijon / 8:23 A.M.

   _____

SCORE _____

TOTAL SCORE _____ /30

2 Bienvenue à Chartres!

Alternative Quiz 2-1A

Maximum Score: 30/100

■ PREMIERE ETAPE

Grammar and Vocabulary

A. You're among a swarm of reporters interviewing a new teenage star. Unfortunately, there is a lot of noise and you can't hear all their questions. Based on the celebrity's answers, write the questions using **est-ce que.** (10 points)

1. Oui, je travaille beaucoup.

   _____

2. Non, ma copine n'aime pas le cinéma.

   _____

3. Oui, je fais de la natation tous les jours.

   _____

4. Oui, nous allons à la plage tous les jours.

   _____

5. Non, je ne joue pas au tennis.

   _____

SCORE [   ]

B. Your French grandmother has just arrived from France, and your mother is welcoming her to your home. Match your mother's question or comment with your grandmother's response. (10 points)

_____ 1. Pas trop fatigué?   **a.** Si, j'ai très soif.

_____ 2. Faites comme chez vous.   **b.** Oui, excellent.

_____ 3. Vous n'avez pas faim?   **c.** Si, je suis crevée.

_____ 4. Vous avez fait bon voyage? **d.** C'est gentil de votre part.

_____ 5. Bienvenue chez nous.   **e.** Merci.

                                        f. Si, je meurs de faim.

SCORE [   ]

Alternative Quiz 2-1A

C. You're going to spend the summer in France, and you are testing your French skills in different situations. How would you respond in each of these situations? (10 points)

1. You are at home and an invited guest knocks at the door. You open the door and say. . .

   _____

2. Your friends just arrived from a long trip to visit you and you want to know how their trip was.

   _____

3. Your friend just said he's dying of thirst. What did you ask him?

   _____

4. You go to a friend's house. His mother opens the door and welcomes you.

   _____

5. She tells you to make yourself at home.

   _____

SCORE [   ]

TOTAL SCORE [/30]

Holt French 2 Allez, viens!, Chapter 2

CHAPITRE 2

CHAPITRE 2

2 Bienvenue à Chartres!

Alternative Quiz 2-2A

■ DEUXIEME ETAPE

Maximum Score: 35/100

Grammar and Vocabulary

A. Your sister Elodie is writing a letter to her friend in Morocco, describing her room. Help her complete the letter with the appropriate forms of the adjectives in parentheses. (10 points)

> Salut Tarek,
>
> Voilà quelques photos de notre maison et de ma chambre. Comme tu vois, c'est une
> **(1)** _____ (grand) maison avec un
> **(2)** _____ (grand) jardin. Ma chambre est au
> premier étage, et elle a une **(3)** _____ (petit)
> terrasse privée. Dans ma chambre, il y a un **(4)** _____
> (petit) lit, une **(5)** _____ (vieux) armoire, deux
> **(6)** _____ (beau) posters, une
> **(7)** _____ (grande) étagère et un bureau. Sur
> mon bureau, il y a un **(8)** _____ (nouveau)
> ordinateur et une **(9)** _____ (joli) lampe rouge.
> Ah oui, voilà ma **(10)** _____ (nouveau) chaîne-
> stéréo près du lit. C'est chouette, non? Et ta maison, elle est comment? Ecris-moi vite!
>   Amitiés,
>   Élodie

SCORE ☐

B. Match the following French words with their English equivalents. (10 points)

_____ 1. le tapis
_____ 2. le jardin
_____ 3. le balcon
_____ 4. la salle de bain
_____ 5. le rez-de-chaussée

a. ground floor
b. shelves
c. bathroom
d. rug
e. restroom
f. yard
g. balcony

SCORE ☐

Alternative Quiz 2-2A

C. Read the following statements and circle **logique** if they are logical or **illogique** if they are illogical. (10 points)

1. Je fais la vaisselle dans la cuisine.   **logique**   **illogique**
2. Je prépare un sandwich dans la salle de bains.   **logique**   **illogique**
3. Je tonds le gazon dans le jardin.   **logique**   **illogique**
4. Le lit est dans la chambre.   **logique**   **illogique**
5. J'étudie dans l'armoire.   **logique**   **illogique**
6. Mes étagères sont dans ma chambre.   **logique**   **illogique**
7. Je déjeune dans la salle à manger.   **logique**   **illogique**
8. Mes vêtements sont sous le tapis.   **logique**   **illogique**
9. Ma sœur regarde la télé dans la salle de bains.   **logique**   **illogique**
10. Les W.-C. sont dans ma chambre.   **logique**   **illogique**

SCORE _____

D. Indicate where you would most likely do each of the following activities. Use each place only once. (5 points)

le salon   la salle de bains   la cuisine   la salle à manger
le jardin   la chambre

1. manger un dîner en famille _____
2. regarder la télé _____
3. dormir _____
4. faire la cuisine _____
5. laver la voiture _____

SCORE _____

TOTAL SCORE _____ /35

CHAPITRE

2 Bienvenue à Chartres!

■ TROISIEME ETAPE

Alternative Quiz 2-3A

Maximum Score: 35/100

Grammar and Vocabulary

A. Your friend, Emilie, wants to do several things today. Tell her where she should go to do each activity or errand. Use the expression **Va...** in your response. (10 points)

1. Il me faut un plan de la ville.

   _____

2. Je veux faire de la natation.

   _____

3. Je veux acheter des timbres.

   _____

4. Je veux voir un film.

   _____

5. Je veux acheter un billet de train pour aller à Madrid.

   _____

SCORE _____

B. Based on what the following people are doing, tell where they probably are by circling the appropriate place. (5 points)

1. Frédérique et Isabelle font du camping.

   a. à l'office de tourisme   **b.** au musée   **c.** au terrain de camping

2. Ils achètent des vêtements.

   a. au centre commercial   **b.** au parc   **c.** à l'église

3. Etienne est en cours de biologie.

   a. au lycée   **b.** au musée   **c.** au parc

4. J'achète des livres.

   a. à la bibliothèque   **b.** à la librarie   **c.** à la boulangerie

5. Edouard et Eric font de la natation.

   a. à l'auberge   **b.** à la piscine   **c.** au musée

SCORE _____

CHAPITRE 2

Alternative Quiz 2-3A

C. Complete each sentence with the appropriate preposition from the box below. (10 points)

1. J'aime manger _____ restaurant.

2. On peut voir un film _____ cinéma.

3. François achète du pain _____ boulangerie.

4. Mes amis font un pique-nique _____ parc.

5. Les jeunes jouent au foot _____ stade.

6. Il y a des plans de la ville _____ office de tourisme.

7. On peut avoir de l'argent _____ banque.

8. Il y a des sculptures _____ musée.

9. On peut dormir _____ auberge de jeunesse.

10. On achète un billet de train _____ gare.

au
à l'
aux
à la

SCORE _____

D. Frédéric is taking a walk in the park, and several people ask him for directions to different places in town. Based on the map below and Frédéric's directions, tell where each person needs to go. (10 points)

1. De la bibliothèque, tournez à gauche dans la rue de la Cathédrale. Tournez à droite dans l'avenue Voltaire. C'est à droite en face de la piscine.

_____

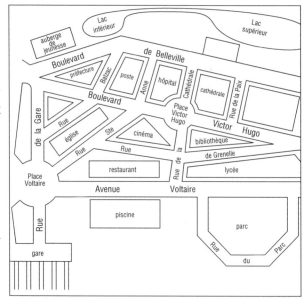

2. De l'auberge de jeunesse, continuez tout droit sur le boulevard de Belleville. Tournez à droite dans la rue de la Paix. Tournez à gauche dans le boulevard Victor Hugo et puis à droite dans la rue de Grenelle. C'est à gauche en face de la bibliothèque.

_____

3. Du parc, vous prenez l'avenue Voltaire. Tournez à droite dans la rue de la Cathédrale. C'est à droite en face de l'hôpital.

_____

4. De la gare, prenez la rue de la gare. Puis, prenez la rue de Ste Anne. C'est à droite juste avant le boulevard Victor Hugo.

_____

5. De la gare, prenez la rue de la gare. Traversez la Place Voltaire et continuez tout droit jusqu'au boulevard Victor Hugo. Tournez à droite sur le boulevard Victor Hugo. C'est à droite en face de la cathèdrale.

_____

SCORE _____

TOTAL SCORE _____ /35

CHAPITRE 2

CHAPITRE 3

Un repas à la française

■ PREMIERE ETAPE

Grammar and Vocabulary

A. Your friend Jeanne is a vegetarian and doesn't eat any meat, including chicken and seafood. Choose four things from the box below that you might buy when you invite her for a meal. (8 points)

une baguette   du pâté

du poulet

des croissants   un bifteck

une tarte aux pommes

des crevettes   du lait

1. _____

2. _____

3. _____

4. _____

SCORE [ ]

B. There is going to be a family reunion at your French host family's house next week, and you're helping out by buying all the groceries. Write three food items you need to buy at each of these stores. (12 points)

LA BOULANGERIE

_____

_____

_____

LA POISSONERIE

_____

_____

_____

LA BOUCHERIE

_____

_____

_____

LA CREMERIE

_____

_____

_____

SCORE [ ]

Alternative Quiz 3-1A

C. You're shopping at an outdoor market in France. Decide if it is **a)** the **vendor** or **b)** the **customer** who is talking. (5 points)

_____ 1. — Combien coûtent les pêches?

_____ 2. — Ça fait 5,10 euros.

_____ 3. — Et avec ça?

_____ 4. — 1,10 euros le kilo. Combien en voulez-vous?

_____ 5. — Je vais en prendre un kilo, s'il vous plaît.

SCORE _____

D. Answer the following questions using the pronoun **en.** (10 points)

1. Tu veux du pâté?

   _____

2. Tu vas prendre 500 grammes de crevettes?

   _____

3. Combien d'œufs est-ce que vous voulez?

   _____

4. On vend du jambon à la charcuterie?

   _____

5. Vous voulez une douzaine d'huîtres?

   _____

SCORE _____

TOTAL SCORE _____ /35

CHAPITRE 3

Un repas à la française

■ DEUXIEME ETAPE

Grammar and Vocabulary

A. You're working part-time for a catering service. Choose the correct expression to complete the following passage about meals in France. (6 points)

Pour le déjeuner et pour **(1)** _____ (le goûter/le dîner), on

commence par **(2)** _____ (une entrée/un dessert). Ensuite, on

sert **(3)** _____ (le fromage/le plat principal) suivi d'

(4) _____ (une salade/une entrée) verte. Après, on passe

(5) _____ (le plat principal/le plateau de fromages). Et pour terminer

le repas, on prend **(6)** _____ (un dessert/une entrée) ou un fruit.

SCORE [   ]

B. You're having dinner with your French host family. Use the articles **un, une, du, de la** or **des** to complete what various people are saying. (9 points)

1. Encore _____ tarte aux fraises?

2. Tu veux _____ poulet?

3. Vous voulez _____ fraises?

4. Tu peux me passer _____ pain, s'il te plaît?

5. Encore _____ rôti?

6. Vous voulez _____ huîtres?

7. Encore _____ escargots?

8. Tu veux _____ viande?

9. Je voudrais _____ religieuse, s'il te plaît.

SCORE [   ]

CHAPITRE 3

Alternative Quiz 3-2A

C. Your French uncle Gilles has given you a list of foods he likes to eat. Use the list to say when he would most likely have each item. (10 points)

> le volaille   les croissants   les religeuses   les mille-feuilles   le bifteck
>
> le lait   les céréales   les fruits de mer   le poisson   la tarte aux fraises

1. Pour le petit déjeuner : _____

2. Comme plat principal : _____

3. Comme dessert : _____

SCORE ☐

D. You're having Christmas dinner with your French host family. What would be the appropriate response to each of the following statements and questions? (10 points)

1. Tu veux des crevettes?

   a. Oui, je veux bien.   **b.** Oui, j'ai soif.   **c.** Voilà.

2. Je pourrais avoir du beurre, s'il vous plaît?

   a. Merci, ça va.   **b.** Tenez.   **c.** Ce n'est pas grand-chose.

3. C'était délicieux.

   a. Je n'ai plus soif.   **b.** C'est gentil.   **c.** Tiens.

4. Encore des huîtres?

   a. Ce n'est pas grand-chose.   **b.** Merci, ça va.   **c.** Voilà.

5. Passez-moi le pâté, s'il vous plaît.

   a. Je n'ai plus faim.   **b.** Oui, je veux bien.   **c.** Voilà.

SCORE ☐

TOTAL SCORE ☐ /35

CHAPITRE 3

CHAPITRE 3

Un repas à la française

Maximum Score: 30/100

■ TROISIEME ETAPE

Grammar and Vocabulary

A. A friend is giving you advice about Christmas gifts for different people. Tell where you'll go to buy each of the gifts your friend suggests. Use complete sentences in your answers. (5 points)

1. Sa mère aime les fleurs.

   _____

2. Tu peux lui offrir un sac à main.

   _____

3. Karine aime les chocolats.

   _____

4. Mme Duchamp a besoin d'un cadre pour une photo.

   _____

5. Grégoire adore les religieuses.

   _____

SCORE ☐

B. You're shopping for greeting cards for the following occasions. Match the wish on the card to the occasion. (5 points)

_____ 1. Your brother broke his leg.　　a. Joyeux anniversaire!

_____ 2. Your cousin Carl got married.　　b. Bonne année!

_____ 3. It's your cousin's birthday.　　c. Meilleurs vœux!

_____ 4. It's Father's Day.　　d. Bonne fête!

_____ 5. Your neighbor is going to London.　　e. Joyeux Noël!

　　　　　f. Bon voyage!

　　　　　g. Bon rétablissement!

SCORE ☐

CHAPITRE 3

Alternative Quiz 3-3A

C. You and your friends are discussing what to give Julie for her birthday. Complete your conversation with the appropriate expressions from the box below. (10 points)

leur	original	déjà	cher	bonne idée	une idée
style	offrons	peut-être	raison	banal	lui

— Tu as **(1)** _____ de cadeau pour Julie?

— **(2)** _____ -lui un portefeuille.

— Non, c'est trop **(3)** _____ . Nous n'avons pas assez d'argent.

— On pourrait **(4)** _____ offrir un disque de Patricia Kaas!

— Non, Elle en a **(5)** _____ un.

— On pourrait lui offrir un bijou. Des boucles d'oreilles **(6)** _____ ?

— C'est **(7)** _____ . En plus, ce n'est pas son

(8) _____ .

— Ecoute, elle adore l'anglais. On pourrait lui offrir un roman en anglais.

— Tu as **(9)** _____ , elle adore l'anglais. Et puis, c'est

(10) _____ comme idée.

SCORE ☐

D. Brigitte and her friends are giving each other advice. To avoid repetition, rewrite the second sentence in each item, using the pronouns **lui** or **leur** as appropriate. (10 points)

1. Tu n'as pas parlé à tes copines depuis trois mois? Téléphone à tes copines demain.

   _____

2. Guillaume va se marier? Tu pourrais offrir un cadre à Guillaume.

   _____

3. Tes parents ont des allergies. N'achète pas de fleurs pour tes parents.

   _____

4. Ton voisin va passer un an à Paris? Offrez un dictionnaire à ton voisin.

   _____

5. Demain, c'est l'anniversaire de mariage mes grands-parents. Qu'est-ce que je peux donner aux grands-parents?

   _____

SCORE ☐

TOTAL SCORE ☐ /30

CHAPITRE 4

Sous les tropiques

PREMIERE ETAPE

Alternative Quiz 4-1A

Maximum Score: 35/100

Grammar and Vocabulary

A. Match the description on the left to the item on the right. (6 points)

_____ 1. Il y a beaucoup de sable.

_____ 2. C'est un morceau de terre au milieu de la mer.

_____ 3. C'est la ville principale d'un pays.

_____ 4. On le trouve au bord de la mer.

_____ 5. Il pleut beaucoup dans cet endroit.

_____ 6. C'est un fruit délicieux.

a. une île

b. un ananas

c. le sable

d. la plage

e. la capitale

f. une forêt tropicale

SCORE _____

B. Complete the following statements about Martinique using an appropriate vocabulary word or expression. (12 points)

1. La Martinique se trouve dans _____ des Caraïbes.

2. La Martinique s'appelle aussi « _____ aux fleurs.»

3. Fort-de-France est _____ de la Martinique.

4. Un _____ est un fruit tropical.

5. On peut voir des champs de _____ à la Martinique.

6. La montagne Pelée est un grand _____ .

SCORE _____

C. Your friend is asking you about your trip to Martinique. Use the adjective in parentheses to answer his questions. Be sure to make all the necessary changes to the adjectives. (12 points)

1. Il y a des villages de pêcheurs? (charmant)

_____

2. Il y a un volcan? (vieux)

_____

Alternative Quiz 4-1A

3. Il y a des moustiques? (gros)

_____

4. Il y a des plages? (beau)

_____

5. Il y a une forêt tropicale? (grand)

_____

6. Il y a des champs de canne à sucre? (grand)

_____

SCORE [   ]

D. An exchange student from Martinique is coming to live in Chicago for a year. He would like to know several things about the city before he comes. Answer each of his questions with the most logical response from the word box below. (5 points)

Elle se trouve dans le nord des Etats-Unis.

Chicago est plus grand que Fort-de-France.

Il y a beaucoup d'activités à faire sur le lac.

Il fait froid.

C'est une ville vivante!

Il fait chaud.

1. Où se trouve cette ville?

_____

2. Qu'est-ce qu'il y a à faire?

_____

3. C'est comment?

_____

4. Quel temps fait-il en hiver?

_____

5. C'est moins grand ou plus grand que Fort-de-France?

_____

SCORE [   ]

TOTAL SCORE [   ] /35

4 Sous les tropiques

■ DEUXIEME ETAPE
Grammar and Vocabulary

Alternative Quiz 4-2A

Maximum Score: 35/100

A. Suggest an activity you might do with your friends for each situation listed below. Be sure to use complete sentences and vary the expressions for suggestions. (12 points)

> **danser le zouk**   **aller à la pêche**   **faire du deltaplane**   **aller se promener**
>
> **faire de la planche à voile**   **se baigner**   **manger des fruits tropicaux**

1. Tarek aime nager.

   _____

2. Hughes et Koffi ont faim.

   _____

3. Nadia et Jérôme adorent manger du poisson.

   _____

4. Marthe veut aller au parc.

   _____

5. Nathalie aime les sports nautiques.

   _____

6. Jean et Mireille aiment la musique.

   _____

SCORE [   ]

B. Paul is talking about what he liked and what he didn't like about his trip to Martinique. Complete his sentences using **ce qui** or **ce que**. (12 points)

1. _____ me plaît, c'est de discuter avec des amis.

2. _____ m'ennuie, c'est de faire du deltaplane.

3. _____ je préfère, c'est déguster des fruits tropicaux.

4. _____ ne me plaît pas, c'est de me lever tôt.

5. _____ j'aime bien, c'est me baigner tout le temps.

6. _____ je n'aime pas, ce sont les moustiques!

SCORE [   ]

Alternative Quiz 4-2A

C. Georges love to try new things, but doesn't know how to swim. Which activities should he do and which ones should he avoid? (6 points)

> faire de la planche à voile
> faire de la plongée sous-marine   danser le zouk
> déguster des fruits tropicaux   se promener   faire de la plongée avec un tuba

Activities to do	Activities to avoid
_____	_____
_____	_____
_____	_____

SCORE [   ]

D. You friend Hervé has written you the following letter from Martinique, telling you about a friend he's made there. Read his letter and circle all the reflexive verbs that you find. (5 points)

Salut de la Martinique!

Hier j'ai rencontré un garçon super cool à Fort-de France. Hafid est algérien et il est étudiant ici. Comme moi, il aime beaucoup faire du sport. Il aime aller à la pêche, se baigner et faire du deltaplane. Demain, on va se lever très tôt pour faire de la plongée. Demain soir, Hafid et moi, nous allons déguster la cuisine martiniquaise avec nos amies Marion et Marie. Puis, on va se promener sur la plage. Il y a beaucoup de choses à faire et à voir à la Martinique... Je m'amuse tellement que je ne veux jamais me coucher!

Hervé

SCORE [   ]

TOTAL SCORE [   ] /35

CHAPITRE 4

4 Sous les tropiques

Alternative Quiz 4-3A

Maximum Score: 30/100

■ TROISIEME ETAPE

Grammar and Vocabulary

A. Séverine is describing her morning routine. Complete her description with the appropriate expressions. (5 points)

1. D'abord, je me lève à six heures du matin et je _____ .
   wash

2. Je _____ avant le petit déjeuner.
   to get dressed

3. Je _____ après le petit déjeuner.
   brush my teeth

4. Je vais au lycée avec mon frère _____ huit heures.
   about

5. En semaine, je _____ à dix heures.
   go to bed

SCORE [   ]

B. Laurent is telling you how often he does the following things. Complete his statements, using the cues provided. (10 points)

1. être en retard (ne... jamais)

   _____

2. se laver le matin (toujours)

   _____

3. se lever à 7 heures (d'habitude)

   _____

4. prendre le petit déjeuner sur la terrasse (souvent)

   _____

5. être encore en pyjama l'après-midi (quelquefois)

   _____

SCORE [   ]

Alternative Quiz 4-3A

C. For each of the following sets of activities, circle the one that Sandrine would logically do first. (5 points)

1. prendre le petit déjeuner / se coucher

2. s'habiller / aller au lycée

3. se brosser les dents / se lever

4. se laver / se lever

5. aller à l'école / se laver

SCORE _____

D. Joseph is describing his family's morning routine. Number the activities in a logical order. (5 points)

_____ On se brosse les dents après le petit déjeuner.

_____ On s'habille avant de prendre le petit déjeuner.

_____ D'habitude, on mange des croissants et des céréales vers huit heures.

_____ On se lève à sept heures.

_____ On se lave avant de s'habiller.

SCORE _____

E. Julien is talking about what he and his friends do on the weekend. Complete each of his statements with the correct reflexive pronoun. (5 points)

1. Elles _____ baignent à la plage.

2. Nous _____ levons tard le dimanche.

3. On _____ promène sur la plage.

4. Je _____ amuse au parc.

5. Tu _____ couches tard le samedi.

me/m'	vous
se	
te	nous

SCORE _____

TOTAL SCORE _____ /30

Quelle journée!

Alternative Quiz 5-1A

Maximum Score: 35/100

■ PREMIERE ETAPE

Grammar and Vocabulary

A. Circle the phrase that logically completes each sentence. (5 points)

1. ... ? Raconte!

   a. Qu'est-ce qui se passe   **b.** Vous n'avez pas faim   **c.** Ça te dit de nager

2. Nous avons reçu... de notre oncle.

   a. le bulletin trimestriel   **b.** une marche   **c.** un cadeau

3. Louis a perdu ses...

   a. devoirs   **b.** livre   **c.** chemise

4. Pauvre Annick, elle... sa nouvelle robe.

   a. a reçu   **b.** a déchiré   **c.** a entendu

5. Samedi dernier, ma mère... un accident.

   a. a eu   **b.** a été   **c.** a fait

SCORE ☐

B. Your friends are telling you about their day. Indicate if they had **a) a good day** or **b) a bad day.** (4 points)

1. _____ Je n'ai pas entendu le réveil.

2. _____ J'ai reçu mon bulletin trimestriel. J'ai eu 3 en français.

3. _____ J'ai eu 18 à mon interro d'anglais.

4. _____ J'ai été collé.

SCORE ☐

Alternative Quiz 5-1A

C. Marius and his friends are talking about what they did last week. Complete the following sentences with the correct form of the verb in parentheses in the **passé composé.** (10 points)

1. Je/J' _____ (boire) du thé.

2. Nous _____ (voir) une pièce de théâtre.

3. Sophie _____ (recevoir) ton bulletin trimestriel.

4. Stéphanie et Susanne _____ (finir) leurs devoirs.

5. Tu _____ (manger) un croque-monsieur.

6. Je/J' _____ (être) collé.

7. Vous _____ (ne pas prendre) le bus pour aller l'école.

8. Tu _____ (perdre) ton dictionnaire.

9. Martin et Mathieu _____ (lire) un roman en espagnol?

10. Marc et Tatiana _____ (ne pas faire) leurs devoirs de maths.

SCORE _____

D. Complete Marc's journal entry about his day by choosing the correct verb and putting it in the **passé composé.** (16 points)

| déchirer | ne pas sonner | avoir | arriver | recevoir |
| passer | | rater | être | tomber |

Je/J' **(1)** _____ une journée épouvantable hier! Mon réveil

(2) _____ . Alors, je/j' **(3)** _____ le bus.

En plus, en sortant du bus, je/j' **(4)** _____ et je/j'

(5) _____ mon pantalon préféré. Je **(6)** _____

en classe avec trente minutes de retard. Je/J' **(7)** _____ une mauvaise

note à mon interro de géographie et donc je/j' **(8)** _____ collé! Quelle

journée!

SCORE _____

TOTAL SCORE _____ /35

Holt French 2 Allez, viens!, Chapter 5

Quelle journée!

Alternative Quiz 5-2A

Maximum Score: 35/100

■ DEUXIEME ETAPE

Grammar and Vocabulary

A. You overhear Valérie's friends telling her about their weekends. Categorize their statements according to whether they had a good weekend or a bad one. (5 points)

Tout a été de travers!

J'ai passé un week-end horrible!

C'était génial!

Quel week-end formidable!

Ça s'est très bien passé!

Un bon week-end

_____

_____

_____

_____

Un mauvais week-end

_____

_____

_____

_____

SCORE _____

B. Véronique is describing what she and some of her friends did last night. Match each person on the left with what they did on the right. (5 points)

_____ 1. Michel, tu t'es...

_____ 2. Paul et moi, nous sommes...

_____ 3. Virginie et Adèle se sont...

_____ 4. Ils se sont ...

_____ 5. Elle est...

a. arrivés en retard au cinéma.

b. amusée à la fête.

c. levé tard.

d. couchées tôt.

e. allée au cinéma.

f. promenés dans le parc.

SCORE _____

CHAPITRE 5

Alternative Quiz 5-2A

C. Your friends are telling you about their day. Would you respond by saying **a) Ça s'est très bien passé** or **b) C'est pas ton jour?** (5 points)

_____ 1. Je suis arrivé en retard en classe!

_____ 2. J'ai été collé!

_____ 3. Je n'ai pas entendu mon réveil ce matin!

_____ 4. J'ai eu 18 à mon interro de géo!

_____ 5. J'ai perdu mon livre de géographie!   SCORE [   ]

D. Agnès has taken some notes about what she and her friends did last weekend. Help her write complete sentences in her journal using the cues provided. Be sure to put the sentences in the **passé composé** and use the correct helping verb, **avoir** or **être** as needed. (20 points)

1. (Moi) se lever tôt ce matin

   _____

2. (Moi) faire mes devoirs

   _____

3. (Mes copains et moi) aller à la plage

   _____

4. Après, (Nous) prendre le bus pour aller chez Paul

   _____

5. (On) arriver de bonne heure chez lui

   _____

6. (Moi) voir un film avec Paul, Nicolas et Aurélie au cinéma

   _____

7. (Nous) aller au café après le film

   _____

8. (Moi) boire une limonade

   _____

9. (Mes copains et moi) bien s'amuser samedi soir

   _____

10. (Moi) se coucher après minuit samedi soir

   _____

SCORE [   ]

TOTAL SCORE [   ] /35

CHAPITRE 5

Quelle journée!

■ TROISIEME ETAPE

Grammar and Vocabulary

A. Complete the following sentences using the cues provided. (10 points)

1. Tu as gagné ton match de tennis! _____ !
   (Congratulations)

2. Tu es encore en retard! _____ .
   (Don't do it again)

3. Tu as eu 18 en anglais! _____ !
   (Well done)

4. Les sciences naturelles, _____ .
   (isn't my best subject)

5. Pierre est _____ en géo.
   (pretty good)

SCORE [   ]

B. Blandine is talking about her report card. Decide if her statements are **(v) vrai** or **(f) faux** based on her report card below. (10 points)

_____ 1. C'est en éducation physique que je suis la meilleure.

_____ 2. Je ne suis pas douée pour les arts plastiques.

_____ 3. Les maths, ce n'est pas mon fort!

_____ 4. Je suis douée pour l'histoire!

_____ 5. Je suis assez bonne en sciences naturelles.

Anglais	10
Histoire	18
Sc. Naturelles	16
Arts plastiques	10
Maths	17
Éducation physique	16

SCORE [   ]

CHAPITRE 5

Alternative Quiz 5-3A

C. Your classmates are all telling their parents about their last English quiz. Complete their statements and their parents' resonses with a logical vocabulary word or expression from the word box below. (10 points)

mieux	doué	félicitation	facile	Courage	fort
bon	mal	Bravo	le meilleur	le clown	inadmissible

1. — Le français, c'est _____ ! J'ai eu 17 à mon interro.

   — Tu as eu 17 à l'interro? _____ !

2. — Je ne suis pas _____ pour la biologie.

   Tu dois _____ travailler en classe.

3. — Je suis le _____ de la classe en anglais.

   — _____ !

4. — L'informatique, ce n'est pas mon _____ .

   — _____ ! On peut étudier ensemble, si tu veux.

5. — J'ai du _____ à comprendre le professeur.

   — 8 en anglais? C'est _____ .

SCORE [ ]

TOTAL SCORE [ ] /30

CHAPITRE 5

A nous les châteaux!

■ PREMIERE ETAPE

Grammar and Vocabulary

A. Circle the phrase that could <u>not</u> logically complete each sentence. (8 points)

1. Je suis...

    a. allé au zoo.   **b.** donné à manger aux animaux.   **c.** monté dans des tours.

2. Philippe a fait un tour...

    a. dans des tours.   **b.** sur la grande roue.   **c.** sur les montagnes russes.

3. Je suis allé...

    a. au zoo.   **b.** au parc d'attractions.   **c.** un circuit des châteaux.

4. J'ai fait...

    a. un spectacle son et lumière.   **b.** un pique-nique.   **c.** une visite guidée.

SCORE [   ]

B. Raphaël and Raoul are talking about what they did on vacation. Decide if their statements are
a) logique or **b) illogique.** (6 points)

_____ 1. Raphaël a assisté à un spectacle son et lumière au château.

_____ 2. On a fait un pique-nique au parc.

_____ 3. J'ai donné à manger aux animaux au zoo.

_____ 4. J'ai fait une visite guidée dans un château.

_____ 5. Raoul a fait une visite guidée au café.

_____ 6. Nous avons fait un tour sur les montagnes russes.

SCORE [   ]

CHAPITRE 6

Alternative Quiz 6-1A

C. You're a tour guide at a hotel and you're planning possible day trips for your customers. Write two activities that can be done at each place. (12 points)

Au zoo   **Pendant un circuit des châteaux**

_____   _____

_____   _____

Au parc d'attractions

_____

_____

SCORE [   ]

D. You asked your friends about their weekends. According to their responses, did each of them have **a) a good time, b) a fair time** or **c) a bad time.** (9 points)

_____ 1. — Je me suis ennuyée.

_____ 2. — Plus ou moins.

_____ 3. — C'était incroyable!

_____ 4. — Mouais.

_____ 5. — Sûrement pas.

_____ 6. — C'était assez bien.

_____ 7. — Ça m'a beaucoup plu.

_____ 8. — C'était sinistre.

_____ 9. — C'était magnifique!

SCORE [   ]

TOTAL SCORE [   ] /35

Holt French 2 Allez, viens!, Chapter 6

CHAPITRE 6

A nous les châteaux!

DEUXIEME ETAPE

Maximum Score: 35/100

Grammar and Vocabulary

A. You visited a **château** last weekend with some friends. Write complete sentences to tell what you did. Be sure to put the verbs in the **passé composé**. (12 points)

1. au château / à 10h00 / arriver / on / dimanche

   _____

2. monter / je / dans la tour

   _____

3. faire / je / la visite guidée / avec Rémi, Julie et Anne

   _____

4. ne pas / Rémi / assister / au spectacle son et lumière

   _____

5. Rémi / rentrer / avant nous / chez lui

   _____

6. très fatigués / nous / rentrer

   _____

SCORE [____]

B. Céline, Rachel, and Christelle had a very busy afternoon. Complete the following sentences about what they did, using the correct past participle from the choices provided. (7 points)

1. Elles sont _____ de la maison de bonne heure.
   parties   parti   partis

2. Céline, Rachel et Christelle ont _____ l'autobus.
   attendus   attendu   attendue

3. Au lycée, Céline est _____ dans l'escalier.
   tombée   tombés   tombé

4. Céline, Rachel et Christelle sont _____ à la maison après les cours.
   rentrés   rentrée   rentrées

5. Plus tard, Rachel est _____ au café avec des amis.
   allés   allée   allé

6. Rachel et ses amies sont _____ pendant deux heures au café.
   resté   restée   restés

CHAPITRE 6

Alternative Quiz 6-2A

7. Céline et Christelle sont _____ dans la chambre de Christelle pour étudier.

montée   montées   montés

SCORE [ ]

C. Corinne is writing a postcard home about her trip to Chenonceaux. Help her complete the postcard by putting the verbs in parentheses in the **passé composé**. (10 points)

Chère Maman,

On **(1)** _____ beaucoup _____ (s'amuser) à Chenonceaux.
Nous **(2)** _____ (visiter) le château hier. Le bus **(3)** _____
(partir) de bonne heure. Sébastien **(4)** _____ (ne pas arriver) à l'heure et il
(5) _____ (rater) le bus. Et moi, quand je **(6)** _____
(descendre) du bus, je **(7)** _____ (tomber)! Plus tard, pendant la visite du
château, Stéphane et Thierry **(8)** _____ (monter) dans les tours. Le midi, nous
(9) _____ (manger) au restaurant et puis nous **(10)** _____
(retourner) à l'hôtel assez tard. C'était génial

                    Je t'embrasse,
                    Corinne

SCORE [ ]

D. Tonio tells a lot of tall tales. Throughout the day, you hear him tell the following extraordinary things to friends. Complete his friends' responses, using each word or phrase only once. (6 points)

1. — J'ai mangé vingt pains au chocolat pour le petit déjeuner.

    — Tu _____ !

2. — Je parle italien et allemand.

    — Ça _____ !

3. — Il y a dix interros en anglais aujourd'hui.

    — N'importe _____ !

4. — J'ai trouvé mille euros dans la rue.

    — C'est pas _____ !

5. — J'ai vu Vanesa Paradis à la boulangerie hier.

    — Pas _____ !

6. — J'ai rencontré le président des Etats-Unis le week-end dernier.

    — Mon _____ !

plaisantes

œil

possible

m'étonnerait

vrai

quoi

SCORE [ ]

TOTAL SCORE [ ] /35

TROISIEME ETAPE

Grammar and Vocabulary

A. You're in a train station and overhear bits of conversations. Decide if what you hear would be said by **a) a traveler** or **b) an employee.** (10 points)

_____ 1. — Vous fermez quand?

_____ 2. — C'est combien un aller-retour Paris-Nantes?

_____ 3. — Ça coûte 20 euros.

_____ 4. — Vous voulez un aller simple?

_____ 5. — Alors, je voudrais un aller-retour, s'il vous plaît.

_____ 6. — 40 euros, madame.

_____ 7. — Du quai 3.

_____ 8. — Bon voyage!

_____ 9. — A quelle heure est-ce que le train pour Lyon part?

_____ 10. — A dix heures, monsieur.

SCORE ☐

B. Complete the following statements with the correct present tense form of the verb **ouvrir.** (6 points)

1. Le magasin n' _____ pas avant dix heures.

2. A quelle heure est-ce que la poste _____ ?

3. Est-ce qu'ils _____ vers 8h30.

4. Nous _____ nos portes à neuf heures.

5. J' _____ toujours de bonne heure?

6. Les magasins _____ généralement vers neuf heures.

SCORE ☐

CHAPITRE 6

Alternative Quiz 6-3A

C. Match the responses on the left with the appropriate question on the right. (4 points)

_____ 1. A 7h30, madame.

_____ 2. 35 euros.

_____ 3. Du quai 8.

_____ 4. Il part à 8h53.

a. A quelle heure est-ce que le train pour Paris part?

b. Combien coûte un aller-retour Marseille-Lyon ?

c. A quelle heure est-ce que vous ouvrez?

d. De quel quai?

SCORE _____

D. Vincent needs to buy some train tickets. Help him reword his questions more formally using **est-ce que**, to ask the train employee for the following information. (10 points)

1. Combien coûte le billet?

_____

2. Le train part à quelle heure?

_____

3. Vous ouvrez à quelle heure?

_____

4. Le train part quand?

_____

5. Combien coûte un aller-retour?

_____

SCORE _____

TOTAL SCORE _____ /30

CHAPITRE 6

CHAPITRE 7

En pleine forme

PREMIERE ETAPE

Grammar and Vocabulary

A. Alexandre and his friends are at summer camp. Help him complete his notes about everything his friends did by choosing the appropriate form of the verb from the given choices. (5 points)

1. Isabelle s'est _____ le bras hier.
   cassé   cassée   cassées

2. Antoine s'est _____ mal au genou en jouant au football.
   fait   faite   faits

3. Samedi, Cédric s'est _____ vers dix heures!
   levé   levées   levés

4. Eric s'est _____ le doigt.
   coupé   coupée   coupées

5. Frédérique s'est _____ la cheville.
   foulée   foulé   foulés

SCORE [   ]

B. You're the school nurse. Complete the following student complaints using an expression from the box below. (12 points)

| bien | à l'oreille | un rhume | à la gorge | au cœur |
| à la tête | malade | éternue | partout |

1. — J'ai beaucoup chanté pendant le concert hier et j'ai mal _____ .

2. — J'ai mal _____ . J'ai besoin d'aspirine.

3. — J'ai mangé trop de chocolat. J'ai mal _____ .

4. — J'ai joué au tennis hier et maintenant j'ai mal _____ .

5. — J'ai des allergies. J' _____ beaucoup.

6. — J'ai la grippe. Je suis _____ .

SCORE [   ]

Alternative Quiz 7-1A

C. Circle the phrase that does not logically complete each sentence. (5 points)

1. J'ai mal...

   a. la grippe.   **b.** partout.   **c.** aux dents.

2. Je suis...

   a. tout raplapla.   **b.** en forme.   **c.** de la fièvre.

3. J'ai...

   a. malade.   **b.** le nez qui coule.   **c.** mal dormi.

4. Je me suis cassé...

   a. le nez.   **b.** un rhume.   **c.** le bras.

5. ... le doigt.

   a. Je me suis foulé   **b.** Je me suis coupé   **c.** Je me suis fait mal

SCORE _____

D. You need to go to the doctor but aren't sure how to say what is wrong with you. Match the French expression on the left to its English equivalent on the right. (5 points)

_____ 1. l'oreille   **a.** fever

_____ 2. la dent   **b.** a cold

_____ 3. le cou   **c.** the neck

_____ 4. un rhume   **d.** the tooth

_____ 5. la fièvre   **e.** the arm

                              f. the ear

SCORE _____

E. Delphine is going to the pharmacy to buy some things for her friends. Based on Delphine's list, write a complete sentence to tell what's wrong with her friends. (8 points)

1. aspirin   Denise et Alain _____ .

2. crutches   Dominique _____ .

3. throat lozenges Hélène _____ .

4. tissues   Albert et Elodie _____ .

SCORE _____

TOTAL SCORE _____ /35

7 En pleine forme

■ **DEUXIEME ETAPE**

Grammar and Vocabulary

A. Charles is training with a French coach for the triathalon. Help him make a list , for his coach, of four things he does at the gym to strengthen himself and stay fit. (8 points)

1. _____
2. _____
3. _____
4. _____

SCORE ☐

B. You're coaching French teenagers at a sports camp. Read the following snippets of conversations and tell whether the speaker is **a) giving advice, b) accepting advice,** or **c) rejecting advice.** (9 points)

1. _____ **Non, je n'ai pas très envie.**

2. _____ **Pourquoi tu ne fais pas de la natation?**

3. _____ **Je n'ai pas le temps.**

4. _____ **D'accord.**

5. _____ **Tu devrais faire du jogging.**

6. _____ **Tu n'as qu'à faire de l'exercice.**

7. _____ **Ce n'est pas mon truc.**

8. _____ **Pas question!**

9. _____ **Tu as raison.**

SCORE ☐

C. Jeanne is doing a survey on how often students exercise. Write complete sentences, using the cues provided, to report the results. (5 points)

1. Julie / push-ups / never

   _____

2. Christian et Sophie / gymnastics / 3 times a week

   _____

3. I / lift weights / everyday

   _____

4. Daniel and David / sit-ups / sometimes

_____

5. Karine et moi / aerobics / every Monday

_____

SCORE [   ]

D. Laetitia is encouraging her friend Eric to complete his workout. Complete their conversation with an appropriate expression from the box. (7 points)

presque	mon truc	raplapla	envie	raison
un effort	Encore	pourquoi	en peux	

— Laetitia, je n' **(1)** _____ plus! Je me sens tout

(2) _____ .

— **(3)** _____ un effort! Tu y es **(4)** _____ !

Tu n'as qu'à faire de l'exercice plus souvent, des pompes ou même de l'aérobic.

— Mais non, je n'ai pas **(5)** _____ . Ce n'est pas

(6) _____ .

— Ecoute, demain, tu viens avec moi. On va jouer au basket. Tu vas t'amuser!

— Tu as **(7)** _____ . On y va demain.

SCORE [   ]

E. Use the present tense form of the verb **devoir** to give your friends advice about different things. (6 points)

1. Nous _____ téléphoner à leurs parents.

2. Vous _____ faire de la natation l'après-midi.

3. Tu _____ jouer au basket-ball.

4. Ils _____ ranger leur chambre.

5. Je ne _____ pas tondre la pelouse.

6. Edouard ne _____ pas se coucher trop tard.

SCORE [   ]

TOTAL SCORE [   ] /35

Nom _____ Classe _____ Date _____

7 En pleine forme

TROISIEME ETAPE

Maximum Score: 30/100

Grammar and Vocabulary

A. You're an intern at a nutrition center, and you're conducting a workshop about eating habits. Use the verb **se nourrir** to complete the participants' statements about eating well **(bien)** or badly **(mal)**. (6 points)

1. Ma copine boit beaucoup d'eau chaque jour.

    Elle _____.

2. Laurence, tu aimes manger des pâtes et une salade.

    Tu _____.

3. Vous mangez beaucoup de hamburgers et de frites.

    Vous _____.

4. Je mange des chips entre les repas!

    Je _____.

5. Ils sautent souvent le petit déjeuner.

    Ils _____.

6. Nous mettons trop de sel dans tous les plats.

    Nous _____.

SCORE [   ]

B. You want to follow a healthy diet. Make two lists to post on your refrigerator to remind you of things to do and things to avoid. (16 points)

JE DOIS...
1. _____
2. _____
3. _____
4. _____

JE DOIS EVITER DE...
1. _____
2. _____
3. _____
4. _____

SCORE [   ]

Alternative Quiz 7-3A

C. Etienne and François are discussing eating habits. Complete their conversation using an expression from the box below. Use each expression only once. (8 points)

> devrais   doit   matières grasses   repas   évite   fruits
>
> sautes   se nourrir
>
> consomme   suivre   bon pour la santé   meilleur que   grignotes

ETIENNE   Tu **(1)** _____ trop entre les repas Didier!

FRANÇOIS   Mais je mange du pain. C'est **(2)** _____ des chips!

ETIENNE   C'est vrai, mais tu **(3)** _____ les repas et tu ne manges pas

de **(4)** _____ . Ce n'est pas

(5) _____ !

FRANÇOIS   Oui, mais par contre, je ne **(6)** _____ jamais trop de sucre

ou de **(7)** _____ .

ETIENNE   Peut-être. Mais tu **(8)** _____ mieux te nourrir.

SCORE [   ]

TOTAL SCORE [   ] /30

Nom_____ Classe_____ Date_____

C'était comme ça

■ PREMIERE ETAPE

Maximum Score: 30/100

Grammar and Vocabulary

A. Koffi just moved to the country but misses city life. Help him complete his journal entry by filling in the blanks with the correct imperfect form of the verb in parentheses. (5 points)

Je regrette beaucoup ma vie à la ville. Je/J' **(1)** _____ (avoir) beaucoup

d'amis au lycée. Mon frère et moi, nous **(2)** _____ (avoir) des boums chez

nous et mes parents **(3)** _____ (être) plus heureux aussi.

C' **(4)** _____ (être) toujours animé et il y **(5)** _____

(avoir) toujours quelque chose à faire. La ville me manque.

SCORE [____]

B. Frédéric and his friends are talking about things that they miss. Match each person's situation with the statement he or she made. (4 points)

_____ 1. Gilles just moved to a big city.

_____ 2. Louise's best friend just moved away.

_____ 3. Kyle is from Quebec and has just arrived in Tahiti.

_____ 4. Grégoire's parents are away on a trip.

a. — Ce qui me manque, c'est la cuisine américaine.

b. — Mes parents me manquent.

c. — Ma meilleure amie me manque.

d. — Ce qui me manque, c'est la neige.

e. — Je regrette la campagne.

SCORE [____]

C. Georges just moved from the city to the country and he's discussing his experiences with his new friend, Hervé. Complete their conversation with the appropriate word or expression from the box below. (8 points)

> Il y avait   ce qui me manque   fais-toi   c'était   comment   regrette
> propre   tellement   mortel   voir que

— Tu sais, Hervé, je **(1)** _____ la vie à la ville.

— C'était **(2)** _____ différent?

Alternative Quiz 8-1A

— Oui, la ville était animée et très vivante. Il y avait toujours quelque chose à faire.

(3) _____ beaucoup de jolies maisons partout.

— Mais la campagne, c'est intéressant aussi! Tu vas (4) _____ tout le

monde est gentil ici. Il y a beaucoup de choses à faire à la campagne aussi.

— Mais non, c'est (5) _____ . Je n'ai pas beaucoup d'amis et il n'y a

pas de fêtes!

— Ecoute, Georges, (6) _____ une raison. La vie est plus simple.

C'est (7) _____ et relaxant ici.

— Tu as raison. La ville, (8) _____ trop bruyant.

SCORE [   ]

D. Guillaume is comparing the pros and cons of country life and city life. Write four statements
that he might make about each place. (8 points)

la campagne	la ville
_____	_____
_____	_____
_____	_____
_____	_____

SCORE [   ]

E. Hughes' grandmother is talking about her life. Read each sentence and decide if she is talking
about **a) her life now** or **b) her life 50 years ago.** (5 points)

_____ 1. Il y a toujours beaucoup à faire.

_____ 2. On avait deux chats chez nous.

_____ 3. C'est très vivant en ville.

_____ 4. La vie était moins stressante.

_____ 5. Il y avait beaucoup de jolies maisons.

SCORE [   ]

TOTAL SCORE [/30   ]

Holt French 2 Allez, viens!, Chapter 8

CHAPITRE

8 C'était comme ça

Alternative Quiz 8-2A
Maximum Score: 35/100

■ DEUXIEME ETAPE

Grammar and Vocabulary

A. Jean and Jérôme are talking about their childhood. Jean was a well-behaved child, but Jérôme was not. Using expressions from the box below, write eight sentences, four in which Jean describes what he was like, and four in which Jérôme describes how he was. Include additional details as appropriate. (16 points)

> ne pas faire de bêtises   aider mon père   être difficile   faire le ménage
> taquiner mes sœurs   ne pas avoir de responsabilités
> ennuyer ma mère   faire la sieste

Jean

_____
_____
_____

Jérôme

_____
_____
_____
_____

SCORE _____

B. Rearrange the following scrambled sentences that tell what Joseph's family's life used to be like. Be sure to make any necessary changes. (10 points)

1. dur / travailler / mon père

_____

2. des / sœurs / faire / bêtises / mes

_____

3. ne / nous / avoir / pas / soucis / de

_____

4. voiture / petit / quand / être / je / mon / une / conduire / super / père

_____

5. aller / je / l'école / tous les jours / à

_____

SCORE [   ]

C. Some things never change. Tell how the following people used to be when they were young, based on how they are now. (9 points)

1. Nous jouons avec nos frères.

_____

2. Tu gardes ton petit frère.

_____

3. Vous êtes sympas.

_____

4. Elle aide ses amis.

_____

5. Ils ont beaucoup de fêtes.

_____

6. Tu es gentil.

_____

7. Je fais la sieste chaque jour à 1h30.

_____

8. Tu taquines ta sœur.

_____

9. Vous avez beaucoup de responsabilités.

_____

SCORE [   ]

TOTAL SCORE [   ] /35

CHAPITRE 8

C'était comme ça

TROISIEME ETAPE

Grammar and Vocabulary

A. Koffi and Julien and discussing what to do today. Complete their conversation with the appropriate word or expression from the box below. (9 points)

> tissu   un maquis   Je ne veux pas.   bonne idée   du tam-tam   préfère
>
> au marché d'artisans   la mosquée   D'accord   Comme

— Je voudrais acheter quelque chose pour ma sœur. Où est-ce que je peux trouver du

   (1) _____ africain?

— Au marché de Cocody.

— On y va alors?

— **(2)** _____ tu veux.

— J'ai aussi besoin d'acheter un cadeau pour ma mère.

— Qu'est-ce que tu veux lui offrir?

— Je ne sais pas. Si on allait aussi **(3)** _____ ?

— C'est une **(4)** _____ . Il y a souvent des gens qui jouent

   (5) _____ là-bas. Tu as beaucoup de choses à faire aujourd'hui.

— Ce n'est pas tout. J'ai aussi envie de voir la ville. Si on allait visiter

   (6) _____ plus tard cet après-midi? Et après on peut aller manger

   au restaurant.

— Non, je **(7)** _____ manger dans **(8)** _____ .

— **(9)** _____ .

SCORE [   ]

B. You've brought your friends some souvenirs from your trip to Abidjan, but you want to tell them what each object is in French. For each item listed, write the correct French word in the space provided. (12 points)

   1. fabric _____

   2. African drums _____

Alternative Quiz 8-3A

3. mask _____

4. pottery _____

5. basket _____

6. piece of Ivorian cloth _____

SCORE [ ]

C. Your friends all want to do different things today. Make suggestions based on what each one wants to do, using the expression **Si on… ?** Use each expression only once. (14 points)

> écouter de la musique visiter la ville manger dans un maquis
> regarder un match à la télé faire du jogging
> acheter des cadeaux au marché
> faire la sieste jouer du tam-tam aller au marché d'artisans

1. — J'ai envie de déguster la cuisine ivoirienne.

_____

2. — Demain, c'est l'anniversaire de ma mère.

_____

3. — Il y a un bon groupe de musique au café.

_____

4. — Je veux voir un match de foot.

_____

5. — Je n'ai pas bien dormi et je suis tout raplapla.

_____

6. — Je veux acheter des tissus.

_____

7. — J'ai envie de faire de l'exercice.

_____

SCORE [ ]

TOTAL SCORE [ ] /35

CHAPITRE 8

CHAPITRE 9

Tu connais la nouvelle?

▪ PREMIERE ETAPE

Grammar and Vocabulary

A. Circle the word in each group that doesn't belong because of its meaning. (5 points)

1. étonné, mal à l'aise, content, gêné

2. heureux, de bonne humeur, content, étonné

3. amoureux, fâché, de mauvaise humeur, furieux

4. inquiet, gêné, mal à l'aise, amoureux

5. énervé, de bonne humeur, fâché, furieux

SCORE [   ]

B. Describe what each of your friends seemed like based on what happened to them. Use the expression **avoir l'air** + an adjective. (10 points)

▪ amoureux déprimé étonné furieux heureux gêné mal à l'aise inquiet

1. Louis a eu 19 à l'interro de géo.

   _____

2. Lucien et Marc ont perdu leurs devoirs de bio.

   _____

3. Marguerite a reçu un cadeau de ses grands-parents.

   _____

4. Mamadou est allé à la boum de Sandrine mais il n'y connaissait personne.

   _____

5. Laurent est tombé dans la rue.

   _____

SCORE [   ]

CHAPITRE 9

Alternative Quiz 9-1A

C. You're in the lunchroom and overhear parts of other students' conversations. Complete these conversations with the most logical word from the box below. (10 points)

> peut-être   crois   te trompes   voit   raison   l'air contente   à mon avis
>
> ce n'est pas possible!   évidemment   possible   parie   me demande

1. — Pourquoi Sandrine est arrivée en retard?

   — Je _____ qu'elle a perdu ses livres. Elle perd toujours ses affaires.

   — Tu as peut-être _____ .

2. — Je _____ pourquoi Benoît n'est pas en classe aujourd'hui.

   — Je _____ qu'il a raté le bus ce matin.

   — Tu _____ , je l'ai vu descendre de l'autobus devant le lycée ce matin.

3. — Nadia n'était pas de bonne humeur ce matin.

   — _____ , elle a eu une mauvaise note en histoire.

   — _____ . Elle fait toujours le clown en classe.

4. — Pauline n'avait pas _____ ce matin!

   — _____ qu'elle était furieuse. Son petit ami n'est pas venu à leur rendez-vous hier soir.

   — _____ !

   SCORE [   ]

D. Choose the most logical response for each of the statements below. (10 points)

_____ 1. Je crois que Marthe et Koffi se sont disputés.

_____ 2. Je parie que Mireille et Martin sont amoureux.

_____ 3. Je me demande pourquoi Mathieu a l'air déprimé.

_____ 4. A mon avis, Nathalie a l'air inquiète.

_____ 5. Je me demande pourquoi Marie est de bonne humeur?

a. Ce n'est pas possible. Elle est amoureuse de Marius.

b. Tu as peut-être raison. Ils ont l'air de mauvaise humeur.

c. Evidemment. Il y a un examen aujourd'hui et elle n'a pas étudié.

d. A mon avis, elle a reçu un cadeau de son copain.

e. Peut-être qu'il a gagné à la lotterie!

f. Je crois que son chien est mort soudainement.

SCORE [   ]

TOTAL SCORE [   ] /35

CHAPITRE 9

CHAPITRE 9
Tu connais la nouvelle?

■ DEUXIEME ETAPE

Maximum Score: 30/100

Grammar and Vocabulary

A. Stéphanie is writing in her journal but is having trouble saying what she means. How could you say it differently? Rewrite her sentences using another expression to say the same thing as the highlighted expression. (8 points)

1. En rentrant à la maison, **ma voiture est entrée dans une autre voiture.**

_____

2. J'ai **fait la connaissance d'**une fille très sympa à la boum.

_____

3. On **se retrouve** à la piscine à trois heures.

_____

4. Samedi, on se promenait dans la forêt et on **ne savait plus où on était.**

_____

SCORE ☐

B. You haven't seen Séverine all weekend and she has a lot to tell you. Complete her statements using the cues provided. (6 points)

1. La voiture _____ .
   (broke down)

2. Donc je suis rentrée très tard vendredi soir et j'ai été _____ .
   (grounded)

3. Tu _____ ce qui s'est passé à la boum de Guillaume.
   (will never guess)

4. _____ qui est tombé amoureux de Sophie.
   (Guess)

5. Ahmed _____ avec Agnès.
   (broke up with)

6. Maintenant, Mathieu _____ .
   (is sulking)

SCORE ☐

CHAPITRE 9

Alternative Quiz 9-2A

C. Susanne is writing about her weekend in her journal. Complete her entry using the **passé composé** or the **imparfait** of the verbs in parentheses as appropriate. (16 points)

Ce weekend, il **(1)** _____ (faire) beau. J'

(2) _____ (avoir) rendez-vous avec Alexandre.

Malheureusement, l'après-midi, ma voiture

(3) _____ (tomber) en panne. Mes parents

(4) _____ (être) énervés. Ils

(5) _____ (ne pas vouloir) me prêter leur voiture.

Alors, je/j' **(6)** _____ (devoir) rester à la maison.

Je/J' **(7)** _____ (téléphoner) à Alexandre pour lui

expliquer mais il **(8)** _____ (être) très fâché. Nous

(9) _____ (se disputer) et on

(10) _____ (casser). Dimanche matin, Thérèse et

moi, nous **(11)** _____ (voir) Alexandre au café. Il

(12) _____ (faire) la tête. Je lui

(13) _____ (parler) et nous

(14) _____ (décider) d'aller au cinéma ensemble ce

soir. Mais, Alexandre **(15)** _____ (ne pas avoir)

l'air très content. Enfin, je/j' **(16)** _____ (passer) un

week-end assez stressant!

SCORE [____]

TOTAL SCORE [___/30]

CHAPITRE 9

CHAPITRE

9 Tu connais la nouvelle?

■ TROISIEME ETAPE

Maximum Score: 35/100

Grammar and Vocabulary

A. Tell what the following people were busy doing when it started raining. Use the expression **être en train de** + infinitive. (10 points)

1. Pascale et Julie / faire une promenade

   _____

2. Tes parents / regarder la télé

   _____

3. Je / tondre le gazon

   _____

4. Nous / prendre un bain de soleil

   _____

5. Nicolas / jouer au tennis

   _____

   SCORE [   ]

B. Use the verbs below to write a sentence describing what you were doing when something else happened. (10 points)

1. faire une promenade / voir un accident

   _____

2. regarder la télé / Valérie / arriver

   _____

3. travailler au café / rencontrer une fille sympa

   _____

4. monter l'escalier / tomber

   _____

5. se laver / le téléphone / sonner

   _____

   SCORE [   ]

CHAPITRE 9

Alternative Quiz 9-3A

C. Olivier and Paul are talking on the phone about what they did last weekend. Complete their conversation with the appropriate expressions from the box below. (5 points)

heureusement	tu vois	à propos	donc
malheureusement	c'est-à-dire que		à ce moment-là

— (1) _____ , Paul, qu'est-ce que tu as fait ce weekend?

— Je suis allé à une boum vendredi avec Valérie. Malheureusement, mon père n'a pas pu me

prêter sa voiture. (2) _____ , il faisait beau et on y est allés à pied.

— J'ai entendu dire que c'était une boum incroyable! Vous vous êtes bien amusés?

— (3) _____ , non. Quand on est arrivés, tout le monde dansait et

s'amusait. (4) _____ j'ai invité Valérie à danser avec moi mais elle

n'a pas voulu.

— Et alors?

— Alors, Valérie a dit qu'elle devait rentrer avant onze heures.

(5) _____ je me suis fâché parce que je n'ai pas du tout dansé.

Puis on est rentré à pied et il a commencé à pleuvoir!

SCORE [____]

D. Your French teacher has heard all kinds of excuses for not having the homework done on time. Choose the best word or expression to complete the following explanations. (10 points)

1. J'allais à l'école quand mon sac _____ dans la boue.
   a. est tombé   **b.** tombais   **c.** tombe

2. J' _____ en train de faire mes devoirs quand ma maison a pris feu.
   a. suis   **b.** étais   **c.** ai été

3. Je _____ quand mon chien a mangé mes devoirs.
   a. vais dormir   **b.** dormais   **c.** ai dormi

4. Je _____ mes devoirs dans la salle à manger quand j'ai vu un extra-terrestre dans le jardin.
   a. fais   **b.** faisais   **c.** ai fait

5. Je rentrais à la maison pour faire mes devoirs quand la voiture _____ en panne.
   a. tombait   **b.** tombe   **c.** est tombée

SCORE [____]

TOTAL SCORE [____] /35

10 Je peux te parler?

PREMIERE ETAPE

Grammar and Vocabulary

Alternative Quiz 10-1A

Maximum Score: 35/100

A. Your friends are always asking you for advice. Based on each situation, tell your friend what you think he or she should do. Be sure to use **le, la, lui,** or **leur** in your answers. (10 points)

1. J'ai eu une mauvaise note en espagnol et mes parents m'ont privé de sortie.

   _____

2. Il y a une fille dans ma classe que j'aime mais elle ne le sait pas.

   _____

3. J'ai cassé les deux CD préférés de mon frère.

   _____

4. Je me suis disputé avec mon copain hier et il ne me parle plus.

   _____

5. Je suis tombée amoureuse d'un garçon qui habite au Mexique.

   _____

SCORE _____

B. Véronique's car broke down and she missed her date with Pierre. Now he wants to break up and her friends are giving her advice about what to do. Complete their statements with an appropriate word or expression from the box below. Some may be used more than once. (10 points)

pardon	les devoirs	le	téléphone	dis	parle	excuse
réconcilier	ce qui	oublie	lui	expliquer		un cadeau

1. — Tu dois _____ offrir _____ .

2. — _____ -lui que tu l'aimes.

3. — _____ -le!

4. — Je pense que tu devrais te _____ avec lui.

5. — Tu devrais _____ demander _____ .

6. — _____ -toi.

7. — Tu devrais _____ expliquer _____
   s'est passé.

SCORE _____

Alternative Quiz 10-1A

C. Rewrite each of the following sentences, using an object pronoun to replace the underlined portion. (8 points)

1. Téléphone <u>à ta tante</u> ce soir.

   _____

2. Ne parle pas <u>à ton chien</u>.

   _____

3. Explique <u>à Julien</u> ce qui s'est passé.

   _____

4. Tu devrais oublier <u>Christelle</u>.

   _____

5. Invite <u>Céline</u> à la boum.

   _____

6. Je dois demander pardon <u>à mes parents</u>.

   _____

7. Tu dois expliquer <u>à Richard et moi</u> ce qui s'est passé.

   _____

8. Je vais inviter <u>Raoul et Blandine</u> au cinéma.

   _____

SCORE [   ]

D. Philippe has a problem and is asking Virginie for her advice. Place their conversation in the correct order by numbering the following sentences from 1−7. (7 points)

_____ — Alors là, tu dois décider avec qui tu préfères sortir. J'ai une idée. Pourquoi pas demander à Agnès d'aller au cinéma samedi au lieu de vendredi? Comme ça, tu sors avec Aurélie vendredi et Agnès samedi. Bonne idée, n'est-ce pas?

_____ — J'ai un problème et je ne sais pas quoi faire. Aurélie m'a invité à la boum de Raphaël vendredi.

_____ — Génial! Je vais téléphoner à Agnès tout de suite.

_____ — Bien sûr, Philippe. Qu'est-ce qu'il y a?

_____ — Le problème, c'est que j'avais déjà promis à Agnès d'aller au cinéma avec elle vendredi. À ton avis, qu'est-ce que je dois faire?

_____ — Dis, Virginie. Tu as une minute?

_____ — Mais, je ne vois pas le problème.

SCORE [   ]

TOTAL SCORE [   ] /35

10 Je peux te parler?

Alternative Quiz 10-2A

Maximum Score: 35/100

■ DEUXIEME ETAPE

Grammar and Vocabulary

A. You're hosting a francophone gala next week at your house. Your friend Claudine has offered to help. Make a list of five things you need to do to get ready. (5 points)

Je dois...

1. _____
2. _____
3. _____
4. _____
5. _____

SCORE ☐

B. You're planning a party on Saturday and you ask your friends for help with the preparations. Use a different expression to ask one of them to do each of the following things. (6 points)

1. _____ envoyer les invitations?
2. _____ choisir la musique?
3. _____ faire le ménage?

SCORE ☐

C. You've asked two of your friends, Robert and Sébastien, for help getting ready for the party. Robert agreed to help but Sébastien is making excuses. Write three things each person might say in response to your requests. (12 points)

Robert	Sébastien
_____	_____
_____	_____
_____	_____

SCORE ☐

D. Your parents have told you that you can't go out with your friends until you finish your chores. Based on the cues provided, respond to each of your parents' questions. Be sure to use the appropriate direct object pronouns in your answers. (5 points)

1. Tu as fait tes devoirs?

   (non) _____

2. Tu as envoyé mes lettres?

   (oui) _____

3. Tu as fait la vaisselle?

   (oui) _____

4. Tu as sortie la poubelle?

   (oui) _____

5. Tu as promené le chien?

   (non) _____

SCORE _____

E. Your sister is worried about the preparations for a party she's giving, but Corinne is reassuring her about what's already been done. Based on each of Corinne's responses, circle the letter that tells what your sister asked her about. (7 points)

1. Je l'ai faite.

   a. le ménage   **b.** la vaisselle   **c.** les courses

2. Stéphane l'a acheté.

   a. le cadeau   **b.** la musique   **c.** les fleurs

3. Tes parents les ont envoyés.

   a. les paquets   **b.** les invitations   **c.** la lettre

4. Thierry les a promenés.

   a. le chat   **b.** les chiens   **c.** la voiture

5. Je l'ai invité.

   a. Ali   **b.** Christian et François   **c.** Annie

6. Tonio l'a choisi.

   a. les films   **b.** le disque   **c.** la musique

7. Vous les avez préparés.

   a. le ménage   **b.** les tartes   **c.** les sandwiches

SCORE _____

TOTAL SCORE _____ /35

10 Je peux te parler?

Alternative Quiz 10-3A

Maximum Score: 30/100

■ TROISIEME ETAPE

Grammar and Vocabulary

A. Vincent is always very apologetic when someone reproaches him. Complete his conversations with an appropriate expression from the box below. (16 points)

rien	ma faute	t'en	aurais dû		m'en veux
grave		aurais pu	excuse	désolé	pas de mal

1. — Eh, attention! Tu vas casser mes disques!

   — _____ ! Tu ne _____ pas?

   — C'est pas _____ .

2. — Tu _____ me téléphoner hier pour m'inviter à la boum.

   — _____ -moi. J'étais fatigué et j'ai fait une sieste.

   — Il n'y a _____ . J'ai vu Alain au parc et il m'a invité.

3. — Pourquoi tu es arrivé 30 minutes en retard? J'attends depuis longtemps.

   — C'est de _____ . J' _____ partir plus tôt.

   SCORE [   ]

B. Your friends forgot your birthday yesterday and they've apologized to you. Write four things you can say to accept their apologies. (8 points)

1. _____

2. _____

3. _____

4. _____

   SCORE [   ]

Alternative Quiz 10-3A

C. Your parents are reproaching you for things and you're agreeing with them. Write what you would say based on what your parents said to reproach you, replacing the underlined word with an appropriate object pronoun. (6 points)

1. Tu aurais dû écrire <u>à ton oncle</u>.

   _____

2. Tu aurais dû faire <u>la vaisselle</u>.

   _____

3. Tu aurais dû téléphoner <u>à tes grands-parents</u>.

   _____

4. Tu aurais pu sortir <u>le chien</u>.

   _____

5. Tu aurais dû faire <u>tes devoirs</u>.

   _____

6. Tu n'aurais pas dû faire <u>de sieste</u>.

   _____

SCORE [   ]

TOTAL SCORE [   ] /30

CHAPITRE 11

Chacun ses goûts

PREMIERE ETAPE

Grammar and Vocabulary

A. Identify the following artists or songs. Use the expressions **Il est/Elle est** or **C'est** in your answers. (10 points)

chanteur / chanteuse	canadien(ne)	chanson	américain(e)
français(e)	groupe	antillais(e)	musicienne

1. Zouk Machine

_____

2. Vanessa Paradis

_____

3. *Frère Jacques*

_____

4. Shania Twain

_____

5. Elton john

_____

SCORE _____

B. You and your friends are talking about the new student in your French class. Complete your conversation with the appropriate present tense form of the verb **connaître.** (10 points)

— Cette fille-là, qui est-ce? Je ne la **(1)** _____ pas.

— Elle s'appelle Danielle. Delphine la **(2)** _____ bien.

— Albert et Aurélie la **(3)** _____ . Ils disent qu'elle est sympa. Ils lui ont parlé à la cantine hier.

— Dominique et Hélène, vous **(4)** _____ Danielle aussi?

— Non, nous ne la **(5)** _____ pas encore mais elle a allemand cet après-midi avec nous.

SCORE _____

Alternative Quiz 11-1A

C. Write what kind of music the following people like. (10 points)

1.

Alexandre _____

2.

Elodie _____

3.

Benoît _____

4.

Antoine _____

5.

Emilie _____

SCORE [   ]

TOTAL SCORE [/30]

CHAPITRE 11

Nom _____ Classe _____ Date _____

Chacun ses goûts

DEUXIEME ETAPE

Grammar and Vocabulary

A. Suggest a type of movie to see based on what your friends tell you. Use the expression **Si on** + imparfait in your answers. (12 points)

1. Je m'intéresse beaucoup à toutes choses extra-terrestres!

    _____

2. Je préfère le vieux films français.

    _____

3. J'adore les cow-boys!

    _____

4. J'aime bien les films qui font peur.

    _____

5. Je veux rire.

    _____

6. Je veux voir quelque chose de romantique.

    _____

SCORE [   ]

B. Your friend Frédérique is going to rent a movie, and you're making a list of suggestions. Write, in French, what type of film each of the following is, so that Frédérique will know in which section she should look for them. (10 points)

1. *Les Visiteurs*   _____

2. *Frankenstein*   _____

3. *Indiana Jones et la dernière croisade*   _____

4. *Casablanca*   _____

5. *Nuit blanche à Seatle*   _____

SCORE [   ]

Alternative Quiz 11-2A

C. You're waiting at the bus station, and you overhear part of a conversation in which some people are talking about a movie they want to go see. Complete their conversation logically with an appropriate expression. (8 points)

— Qu'est-ce qu'on **(1)** _____ comme films?

— Ben... Tu veux voir *Dr. Doolittle?*

— Ça commence **(2)** _____ ?

— Euh... A 15h30.

— Ça **(3)** _____ où?

— Au Royal et au Ciné Montparnasse.

— C'est avec **(4)** _____ ?

— C'est avec Eddie Murphy. Il est super.

— D'accord.

SCORE [   ]

D. Choose the word or phrase that best completes the following sentences. (5 points)

1. Ça commence...

   a. au Royal.   **b.** à 13h 30.   **c.** Gérard Depardieu.

2. On joue...

   a. avec Pierce Brosnan.   **b.** au Plumereau.   **c.** Hercule.

3. Ça passe...

   a. à l'Odéon.   **b.** Catherine Deneuve.   **c.** les cowboys

4. Dracula, c'est un film...

   a. d'amour.   **b.** western.   **c.** d'horreur.

5. C'est un film d'action avec...

   a. Le Monde perdu.   **b.** Pierce Brosnan.   **c.** au Gaumont.

SCORE [   ]

TOTAL SCORE [/35]

■ **TROISIEME ETAPE**

Grammar and Vocabulary

A. Jeanne has written a entry in her diary for her French class. Complete it using **qui, que** or **qu'** as appropriate. (10 points)

Hier, j'ai fait la connaissance du garçon **(1)** _____ j'ai vu au café samedi dernier. Il

s'appelle Antonio et il est très sympa. J'ai rendez-vous avec lui dimanche prochain. On va au

cinéma **(2)** _____ se trouve à côté du café. Il m'a dit **(3)** _____ il aimait

les films classiques. Moi aussi, donc, on va voir West Side Story **(4)** _____ passe au

cinéma. J'espère **(5)** _____ Antonio aime aussi danser.

SCORE [   ]

B. Isabelle and Bernard both read the same book over the weekend. Isabelle loved the book, but Bernard didn't. Write three things that each of them might say about the book they read. (18 points)

Isabelle	Bernard
_____	_____
_____	_____
_____	_____
_____	_____

SCORE [   ]

Alternative Quiz 11-3A

C. Your friends are talking about the book that each of them read for a class project. Tell what type of book each person read, based on what they say. (7 points)

1. C'est dans la cinquième scène du premier acte que le héros découvre que Camille est sa sœur.

_____

2. Les Zorkans attaquent la planète et il y a des explosions partout.

_____

3. J'adore Jacques Prévert! Ses poèmes sont tellement intéressants.

_____

4. Max voit Clarice au parc et il tombe tout de suite amoureux.

_____

5. Et puis, tout le village fait une grande fête pour célébrer le retour d'Astérix et Obélix.

_____

6. L'auteur parle de son enfance au Maroc et sa carrière plus tard dans l'armée.

_____

7. Ça parle d'un detective français qui arrive à New York pour chercher un criminel mystérieux qui s'appelle Le Sphinx.

_____

SCORE [____]

TOTAL SCORE [____] /35

Nom_____ Classe_____ Date_____

■ PREMIERE ETAPE

Grammar and Vocabulary

A. Karine and her sister are discussing what they plan to do this weekend. Complete their conversation with a logical expression from the box below. (8 points)

> **se trouve**   **qu'est-ce qu'il y a**   **loups**   **au nord de**   **on peut**
>
> **faire**   **au sud**   **renards**
>
> **faire du camping**   **faire une randonnée en raquettes**

— Dis, Karine, qu'est-ce que tu veux faire ce week-end?

— Je pense aller au parc de la Jacques-Cartier avec mes amis.

— Ah oui? Où **(1)** _____ ce parc?

— C'est **(2)** _____ du lac Saint-Jean.

— **(3)** _____ à voir? Est-ce qu'il y a beaucoup d'animaux?

— Oui, il y a toutes sortes d'animaux comme des **(4)** _____ et des

(5) _____ . Il y a aussi une magnifique forêt à voir.

— Qu'est-ce qu'il y a à **(6)** _____ au parc?

— Beaucoup de choses. On peut **(7)** _____ et

(8) _____ .

— Ça a l'air amusant. Je peux venir aussi?

— Pourquoi pas? Demandons à maman si elle est d'accord.

SCORE _____

B. You and your friends and family are at a campsite and you're planning your activities. Tell what each person is going to do based on what he or she brought. (15 points)

1. Your parents / a mountain bike

_____

2. You / a canoe

_____

Alternative Quiz 12-1A

3. Julie / snow shoes

_____

4. Charles / skis

_____

5. Cédric / hiking boots

_____

SCORE [   ]

C. Your friend is preparing a scrapbook with pictures she took while on her last camping trip. Help her label, in French, the animals in the pictures she took. (12 points)

1.

_____

2.

_____

3.

_____

4.

_____

5.

_____

6.

_____

SCORE [   ]

TOTAL SCORE [   ] /35

12 A la belle étoile

Alternative Quiz 12-2A

Maximum Score: 35/100

■ DEUXIEME ETAPE

Grammar and Vocabulary

A. You and your friends are on a long hiking trip in a national park. Complete the following conversations, using appropriate words or phrases from the box below. (8 points)

> fatigué   presque   meurs   n'en peux   peur
>
> courage   abandonne   crève de faim

1. — Génial! Regardez là-bas. Il y a des ours!

   — Oh non! J'ai _____ des ours!

2. — J' _____ !

   — _____ ! Dix minutes, pas plus.

   — Mais, je n'ai pas mangé avant de partir. Je _____ !

3. — Si on arrêtait un peu? Je suis _____ .

   — On y est _____ .

4. — Tu n'as pas l'air en forme. Qu'est-ce qu'il y a?

   — J'ai oublié d'emporter de l'eau. Je _____ de soif! Je

   _____ plus!

   SCORE [   ]

B. Your friends went camping last weekend but had a terrible time because they forgot some essential items. Based on what went wrong, tell what each of them forgot to bring. (12 points)

1. Je me suis fait piquer par des insectes!

   _____

2. J'ai dû manger de la nourriture froide!

   _____

3. Je n'ai pas bien dormi!

   _____

Alternative Quiz 12-2A

4. Je me suis perdu dans la forêt!

_____

5. Je n'ai pas pu manger de poisson du lac!

_____

6. Je n'ai pas pu bien voir la nuit!

_____

SCORE ☐

C. You're picnicking in the park with some classmates and you see them do the following activities. What advice would you give each of them? (15 points)

1. Christophe coupe les branches d'un arbre.

_____

2. Lætitia donne des chips à un raton laveur.

_____

3. Christian jette des papiers par terre _(on the ground)_.

_____

4. Daniel écrit son nom sur une roche _(rock)_.

_____

5. Laurence s'écarte _(wanders off)_ du sentier.

_____

SCORE ☐

TOTAL SCORE ☐ /35

12 À la belle étoile

■ TROISIEME ETAPE

Alternative Quiz 12-3A

Maximum Score: 30/100

Grammar and Vocabulary

A. Marguerite is camping with friends. Complete her letter to her parents about her trip. Use the **passé composé** or **the imparfait** of the verbs in parentheses as appropriate. (15 points)

> Chers Maman et Papa,
> Je m'amuse bien ici! Il y a beaucoup de choses à faire et à voir. Cet après-midi, il
> **(1)** _____ (faire) beau et je/j' **(2)** _____
> (faire) du canotage avec Marthe. Nous **(3)** _____
> beaucoup _____ (s'amuser) mais l'eau était froide. Mireille
> **(4)** _____ (décider) de faire une randonnée pédestre
> seule. Elle **(5)** _____ (se perdre) parce qu'elle
> **(6)** _____ (ne pas suivre) les sentiers balisés. En
> rentrant, elle **(7)** _____ (être) fatiguée et elle
> **(8)** _____ (avoir) très faim!
> À l'arrivée au camp, il y **(9)** _____ (avoir) du soleil.
> Je/J' **(10)** _____ (faire) du vélo de montagne avec mes amis.
> La première nuit, Marie et moi, nous **(11)** _____ (dormir)
> dans la même tente. Je **(12)** _____ (ne pas emporter) de
> lampe de poche, alors je/j' **(13)** _____ (devoir) emprunter
> celle de Marie. Hier matin, il **(14)** _____ (pleuvoir) et je
> **(15)** _____ (ne pas aller) à la pêche.
>   Je vous embrasse,
>   Marguerite

SCORE [   ]

Alternative Quiz 12-3A

B. M. Delanoë told your French class what his childhood was like. Summarize his talk for the French Club newsletter, using the appropriate **imparfait** forms of the verbs below. (10 points)

1. écouter / toujours de la musique rock
2. jouer / au foot avec des amis
3. ennuyer / mes frères
4. faire souvent / des bêtises
5. mes frères / me taquiner

Quand j'étais petit, _____

_____

_____

_____

_____

_____

_____

_____

SCORE [   ]

C. Mehdi had several things he needed to do to get ready for his camping trip with his friends Louise and Daniel. Rearrange what Mehdi did in a logical order, by numbering his activities from 1−5. (5 points)

_____ Après ça, je suis allé chez Daniel lui donner le sac et voir s'il était prêt à partir.

_____ Après le déjeuner, je suis allé acheter une boussole et un sac de couchage pour Daniel.

_____ Finalement, nous sommes partis vers six heures.

_____ Ensuite, nous sommes rentrés à la maison préparer des sandwiches pour le déjeuner.

_____ D'abord, Louise et moi, nous avons fait les courses.

SCORE [   ]

TOTAL SCORE [   ] /30

Answer Key

Answers to Alternative Quizzes 1-1A, 1-2A, and 1-3A

Alternative Quiz 1-1A

A. (4 points: 1 point per item)
1. Blandine est gourmande.
2. Blandine est jeune.
3. Blandine est brune.
4. Blandine est petite.

B. (12 points: 2 points per item)
Possible answers:
1. Kermit® est vert.
2. Pete Sampras est brun.
3. Le président des Etats-Unis est important.
4. Céline Dion est petite.
5. Answers will vary.
6. Answers will vary.

C. (6 points: 1 point per item)
1. regardons
2. écoutes
3. adorent
4. marche
5. achetez
6. mange

D. (8 points: 1 point per item)
1. ont
2. suis
3. ai
4. sont
5. a
6. est
7. sommes
8. es

Alternative Quiz 1-2A

A. (10 points: 2 points per item)
1. Va acheter un appareil-photo.
2. N'oubliez pas vos passeports.
3. Pense à prendre des photos pendant ton voyage.
4. Ne parlez pas anglais en France.
5. Achète des cartes postales.

B. (10 points: 2 points per item)
1. d
2. b
3. e
4. c
5. a

C. (10 points: 2 points per item)
1. a
2. a
3. a
4. b
5. b

D. (10 points: 2 points per item)
1. un billet d'avion
2. un anorak
3. une écharpe
4. un parapluie/un imperméable
5. des baskets

Alternative Quiz 1-3A

A. (10 points: 2 points per item)
1. Hélène va à la piscine.
2. Je vais au musée.
3. Christophe et Daniel vont au cinéma.
4. Vous allez au restaurant.
5. David et moi, nous allons à la campagne.

B. (4 points: 1 point per item)
3, 4, 1, 2

C. (6 points: 1 point per item)
1. Ça te dit; idée
2. envie; Ça ne me dit
3. pourrait; question

D. (10 points: 2 points per item)
1. Le train de Lille arrive à 11:15.
2. Le train de Biarritz arrive à 22:30.
3. Le train de Toulouse arrive à 16:45.
4. Le train de Poitiers arrive à 19:20.
5. Le train de Dijon arrive à 8:23.

Answers to Alternative Quizzes 2-1A, 2-2A, and 2-3A

Alternative Quiz 2-1A

A. (10 points: 2 points per item)
1. Est-ce que tu travailles beaucoup?
2. Est-ce que ta copine aime le cinéma?
3. Est-ce que tu fais de la natation tous les jours?
4. Est-ce que toi et tes amis allez à la plage?
5. Est-ce que tu joues au tennis?

B. (10 points: 2 points per item)
1. c
2. d/e
3. f
4. b
5. d/e

C. (10 points: 2 points per item)
Possible answers:
1. Bienvenue chez nous/moi!
2. Vous avez fait bon voyage?
3. Tu n'as pas soif?
4. Merci./C'est gentil de votre part.
5. Merci./C'est gentil de votre part.

Alternative Quiz 2-2A

A. (10 points: 1 point per item)
1. grande
2. grand
3. petite
4. petit
5. vieille
6. beaux
7. grande
8. nouvel
9. jolie
10. nouvelle

B. (10 points: 2 points per item)
1. d
2. f
3. g
4. c
5. a

C. (10 points: 1 point per item)
1. L
2. I
3. L
4. L
5. I
6. L
7. L
8. I
9. I
10. I

D. (5 points: 1 point per item)
1. la salle à manger
2. le salon
3. la chambre
4. la cuisine
5. le jardin

Alternative Quiz 2-3A

A. (10 points: 2 points per item)
1. Va à l'office de tourisme.
2. Va à la piscine.
3. Va à la poste.
4. Va au cinéma.
5. Va à la gare.

B. (5 points: 1 point per item)
1. **c.** au terrain de camping
2. **a.** au centre commercial
3. **a.** au lycée
4. **b.** à la librarie
5. **b.** à la piscine

C. (10 points: 1 point per item)
1. au
2. au
3. à la
4. au
5. au
6. à l'
7. à la
8. au
9. à l'
10. à la

D. (10 points: 2 points per item)
1. le restaurant
2. le lycée
3. La cathédrale
4. le cinéma
5. la bibliothèque

Answers to Alternative Quizzes 3-1A, 3-2A, and 3-3A

Alternative Quiz 3-1A

A. (8 points: 2 points per item)
1. des croissants
2. du lait
3. une tarte aux pommes
4. une baguette

B. (12 points: 1 point per item)
Possible answers:
LA BOULANGERIE : des baguettes, des pains au chocolat, des croissants
LA BOUCHERIE : un bifteck, un rôti de bœuf, un poulet
LA POISSONERIE : des crevettes, du poisson, des huîtres
LA CREMERIE : des œufs, du beurre, du fromage

C. (5 points: 1 point per item)
1. b   4. a
2. a   5. b
3. a

D. (10 points: 2 points per item)
Possible answers:
1. Oui, j'en veux.
2. Oui, je vais en prendre 500 grammes.
3. J'en veux une douzaine.
4. Oui, on en vend.
5. Oui, j'en veux une douzaine.

Alternative Quiz 3-2A

A. (6 points: 1 point per item)
1. le dîner
2. une entrée
3. le plat principal
4. une salade
5. le plateau de fromages
6. un dessert

B. (9 points: 1 point per item)
1. de la
2. du
3. des
4. du
5. du
6. des
7. des
8. de la
9. une

C. (10 points: 1 point per item)
1. **Pour le petit déjeuner :** les croissants, les céréales, le lait
2. **Comme plat principal :** la volaille, le bifteck, les fruits de mer, le poisson
3. **Comme dessert :** les religieuses, les mille-feuilles, la tarte aux fraises

D. (10 points: 2 points per item)
1. **a.** Oui, je veux bien.
2. **b.** Tenez.
3. **b.** C'est gentil.
4. **b.** Merci, ça va.
5. **c.** Voilà.

Alternative Quiz 3-3A

A. (5 points: 1 point per item)
1. Je vais aller chez le fleuriste.
2. Je vais aller à la maroquinerie.
3. Je vais aller à la confiserie.
4. Je vais aller à la boutique de cadeaux.
5. Je vais aller à la pâtisserie.

B. (5 points: 1 point per item)
1. g   4. d
2. c   5. f
3. a

C. (10 points: 1 point per item)
1. une idée
2. Offre
3. cher
4. lui
5. déjà
6. peut-être
7. banal
8. style
9. raison
10. original

D. (10 points: 2 points per item)
1. Téléphone leur demain.
2. Tu pourrais lui offrir un cadre.
3. Ne leur achète pas de fleurs.
4. Offrez lui un dictionnaire.
5. Qu'est-ce que je peux leur donner?

Answers to Alternative Quizzes 4-1A, 4-2A, and 4-3A

Alternative Quiz 4-1A

A. (6 points: 1 point per item)
1. d
2. a
3. e
4. c
5. f
6. b

B. (12 points: 2 points per item)
1. la mer
2. l'Ile
3. la capitale
4. answer will vary
5. canne à sucre
6. volcan

C. (12 points: 2 points per item)
1. Oui, il y a de charmants villages de pêcheurs.
2. Oui, il y a un vieux volcan.
3. Oui, il y a de gros moustiques.
4. Oui, il y a de belles plages.
5. Oui, il y a une grande forêt tropicale.
6. Oui, il y a de grands champs de canne à sucre.

D. (5 points: 1 point per item)
1. Elle se trouve dans le nord des Etats-Unis.
2. Il y a beaucoup d'activités à faire sur la lac.
3. C'est une ville vivante!
4. Il fait froid.
5. Chicago est plus grand que Fort-de-France.

Alternative Quiz 4-2A

A. (12 points: 2 points per item)
1. Va te baigner.
2. Mangez des fruits tropicaux.
3. Allez à la pêche.
4. Va te promener.
5. Fais de la planche à voile.
6. Dansez le zouk.

B. (12 points: 2 points per item)
1. Ce qui
2. Ce qui
3. Ce que
4. Ce qui
5. Ce que
6. Ce que

C. (6 points: 1 point per item)
Activities to do: danser le zouk; déguster des fruits tropicaux; se promener
Activities to avoid: faire de la planche à voile; faire de la plongée avec un tuba; faire de la plongée sous-marine

D. (5 points: 1 point per item)
se baigner; se lever; se promener; s'amuser; se coucher

Alternative Quiz 4-3A

A. (5 points: 1 point per item)
1. me lave
2. m'habille
3. me brosse les dents
4. vers
5. me couche

B. (10 points: 2 points per item)
1. Je ne suis jamais en retard.
2. Je me lave toujours le matin.
3. D'habitude, je me lève à 7 heures.
4. Je prends souvent le petit-déjeuner sur la terrasse.
5. Quelquefois, je suis encore en pyjama l'après-midi.

C. (5 points: 1 point per item)
1. prendre le petit déjeuner
2. s'habiller
3. se lever
4. se lever
5. se laver

D. (5 points: 1 point per item)
5, 3, 4, 1, 2

E. (5 points: 1 point per item)
1. se
2. nous
3. se
4. m'
5. te

ANSWERS

Answers to Alternative Quizzes 5-1A, 5-2A, and 5-3A

Alternative Quiz 5-1A

A. (5 points: 1 point per item)
1. **a.** Qu'est-ce qui se passe
2. **c.** un cadeau
3. **a.** ses devoirs
4. **b.** a déchiré
5. **a.** a eu

B. (4 points: 1 point per item)
1. b
2. b
3. a
4. b

C. (10 points: 1 point per item)
1. ai bu
2. avons vu
3. a reçu
4. ont fini
5. as mangé
6. ai été
7. n'avez pas pris
8. as perdu
9. ont lu
10. n'ont pas fait

D. (16 points: 2 points per item)
1. ai passé
2. n'a pas sonné
3. ai raté
4. suis tombé
5. ai déchiré
6. suis arrivé
7. ai eu
8. ai été

Alternative Quiz 5-2A

A. (5 points: 1 point per item)
Un bon week-end: C'était génial!; Ça s'est très bien passé!; Quel week-end formidable!
Un mauvais week-end: Tout a été de travers!; J'ai passé un week-end horrible!

B. (5 points: 1 point per item)
1. c
2. a
3. d
4. f
5. e

C. (5 points: 1 point per item)
1. b
2. b
3. b
4. a
5. b

D. (20 points: 2 points per item)
1. Je me suis levée tôt ce matin.
2. J'ai fait mes devoirs.
3. Mes copains et moi, nous sommes allés à la plage.
4. Après, nous avons pris le bus pour aller chez Paul.
5. On est arrivé de bonne heure chez lui.
6. J'ai vu un film avec Paul, Nicolas et Aurélie.
7. Nous sommes allés au café après le film.
8. J'ai bu une limonade.
9. Nous nous sommes bien amusés samedi soir.
10. Je me suis couchée après minuit samedi soir.

Alternative Quiz 5-3A

A. (10 points: 2 points per item)
1. Félicitations!
2. Ne recommence pas.
3. Chapeau!
4. c'est pas mon fort.
5. assez bon en

B. (10 points: 2 points per item)
1. f
2. v
3. f
4. v
5. v

C. (10 points: 1 point per item)
1. facile / bravo
2. doué / mieux
3. le meilleur / Félicitation
4. fort / Courage
5. mal / inadmissible

Answers to Alternative Quizzes 6-1A, 6-2A, and 6-3A

Alternative Quiz 6-1A

A. (8 points: 2 points per item)
1. **b.** donné à manger aux animaux.
2. **a.** dans des tours.
3. **c.** un circuit des châteaux.
4. **a.** un spectacle son et lumière.

B. (6 points: 1 point per item)
1. L
2. L
3. L
4. L
5. I
6. L

C. (12 points: 2 points per item)
Answer will vary.

D. (9 points: 1 point per item)
1. c
2. b
3. a
4. b
5. c
6. b
7. a
8. c
9. a

Alternative Quiz 6-2A

A. (12 points: 2 points per item)
1. On est arrivés au château dimanche à 10h00.
2. Je suis monté dans la tour.
3. J'ai fait la visite guidée avec Rémi, Julie et Anne.
4. Rémi n'a pas assisté au spectacle son et lumière.
5. Rémi est rentré chez lui avant nous.
6. Nous sommes rentrés très fatigués.

B. (7 points: 1 point per item)
1. parties
2. attendu
3. tombée
4. rentrées
5. allée
6. restées
7. montées

C. (10 points: 1 point per item)
1. s'est [...] amusés
2. avons visité
3. est parti
4. n'est pas arrivé
5. a raté
6. suis descendue
7. suis tombée
8. sont montés
9. avons mangé
10. sommes retournés

D. (6 points: 1 point per item)
1. plaisantes
2. m'étonnerait
3. quoi
4. vrai
5. possible
6. œil

Alternative Quiz 6-3A

A. (10 points: 1 point per item)
1. a   6. b
2. a   7. b
3. b   8. b
4. b   9. a
5. a   10. b

B. (6 points: 1 point per item)
1. ouvre
2. ouvre
3. ouvrent
4. ouvrons
5. ouvre
6. ouvrent

C. (4 points: 1 point per item)
1. c
2. b
3. d
4. a

D. (10 points: 2 points per item)
1. Combien est-ce que le billet coûte?
2. A quelle heure est-ce que le train part?
3. A quelle heure est-ce que vous ouvrez?
4. Quand est-ce que le train part?
5. Combien est-ce qu'un aller-retour coûte?

Answers to Alternative Quizzes 7-1A, 7-2A, and 7-3A

Alternative Quiz 7-1A

A. (5 points: 1 point per item)
   1. cassée
   2. fait
   3. levé
   4. coupé
   5. foulée

B. (12 points: 2 points per item)
   1. à la gorge
   2. à la tête
   3. au cœur
   4. partout
   5. éternue
   6. malade

C. (5 points: 1 point per item)
   1. a. la grippe.
   2. c. de la fièvre.
   3. a. malade.
   4. b. un rhume.
   5. c. Je me suis fait mal

D. (5 points: 1 point per item)
   1. f   4. b
   2. d   5. a
   3. c

E. (8 points: 2 points per item)
   Possible answers :
   1. Denise et Alain ont mal à la tête.
   2. Dominique a mal au pied.
   3. Hélène a mal à la gorge.
   4. Albert et Elodie ont un rhume.

Alternative Quiz 7-2A

A. (8 points: 2 points per item)
   Possible answers:
   1. faire de l'exercice
   2. faire des abdominaux
   3. faire de l'aérobic
   4. faire de la musculation

B. (9 points: 1 point per item)
   1. c   6. a
   2. a   7. c
   3. c   8. c
   4. b   9. b
   5. a

C. (5 points: 1 point per item)
   1. Julie ne fait jamais de pompes.
   2. Christian et Sophie font de la gymnastique trois fois par semaine.
   3. Je fais de la musculation tous les jours.
   4. Daniel et David font quelquefois des abdominaux.
   5. Karine et moi, nous faisons de l'aérobic tous les lundis.

D. (7 points: 1 point per item)
   1. en peux
   2. raplapla
   3. Encore
   4. presque
   5. envie
   6. mon truc
   7. raison

E. (6 points: 1 point per item)
   1. devons
   2. devez
   3. dois
   4. doivent
   5. dois
   6. doit

Alternative Quiz 7-3A

A. (6 points: 1 point per item)
   1. Elle se nourrit bien.
   2. Tu te nourris bien.
   3. Vous vous nourrissez mal.
   4. Je me nourris mal.
   5. Ils se nourrissent mal.
   6. Nous nous nourrissons mal.

B. (16 points: 2 points per item)
   Answers will vary.

C. (8 points: 1 point per item)
   1. grignotes
   2. meilleur que
   3. sautes
   4. fruits
   5. bon pour la santé
   6. consomme
   7. matières grasses
   8. devrais

Answers to Alternative Quizzes 8-1A, 8-2A, and 8-3A

Alternative Quiz 8-1A

A. (5 points: 1 point per item)
1. avais
2. avions
3. étaient
4. était
5. avait

B. (4 points: 1 point per item)
1. e
2. c
3. d
4. b

C. (8 points: 1 point per item)
1. regrette
2. tellement
3. Il y avait
4. voir que
5. mortel
6. fais-toi
7. propre
8. c'était

D. (8 points: 1 point per item)
Answers will vary.

E. (5 points: 1 point per item)
1. a
2. b
3. a
4. b
5. b

Alternative Quiz 8-2A

A. (16 points: 2 points per item)
Possible answers:
Jean : J'aidais mon père avec le travail.
Je ne faisais pas de bêtises.
Je n'ennuyais pas ma mère.
Je faisais le ménage.
Jérôme : Je taquinais mes sœurs.
Je faisais toujours la sieste.
Je n'avais pas de responsa-
bilités.
J'étais difficile.

B. (10 points: 2 points per item)
1. Mon père travaillait dur.
2. Mes sœurs faisaient des bêtises.

3. Nous n'avions pas de soucis.
4. Quand j'étais petit, mon père conduisait une super voiture.
5. J'allais à l'école tous les jours.

C. (9 points: 1 point per item)
1. Nous jouions avec nos frères.
2. Tu gardais ton petit frère.
3. Vous étiez sympas.
4. Elle aidait ses amis.
5. Ils avaient beaucoup de fêtes.
6. Tu étais gentil.
7. Je faisais la sieste chaque jour à 1h30.
8. Tu taquinais ta sœur.
9. Vous aviez beaucoup de respon-sabilités.

Alternative Quiz 8-3A

A. (9 points: 1 point per item)
1. tissu
2. Comme
3. au marché d'artisans
4. bonne idée
5. du tam-tam
6. la mosquée
7. préfère
8. un maquis
9. D'accord

B. (12 points: 2 points per item)
1. tissu
2. des tam-tam
3. un masque
4. une poterie
5. un panier
6. un pagne

C. (14 points: 2 points per item)
1. Si on mangeait dans un maquis.
2. Si on achetait des cadeaux au marché.
3. Si on écoutait de la musique.
4. Si on regardait un match à la télé.
5. Si on faisait la sieste.
6. Si on allait au marché d'artisans.
7. Si on faisait du jogging.

ANSWERS

Answers to Alternative Quizzes 9-1A, 9-2A, and 9-3A

Alternative Quiz 9-1A

A. (5 points: 1 point per item)
1. content
2. étonné
3. amoureux
4. amoureux
5. de bonne humeur

B. (10 points: 2 points per item)
Possible answers:
1. Louis avait l'air heureux.
2. Lucien et Marc avaient l'air inquiet.
3. Marguerite avait l'air étonnée.
4. Mamadou avait l'air mal à l'aise.
5. Laurent avait l'air gêné.

C. (10 points: 1 point per item)
1. crois; raison
2. me demande; parie; te trompes
3. A mon avis; Possible
4. l'air contente; Evidemment; Ce n'est pas possible

D. (10 points: 2 points per item)
1. b   2. a   3. f   4. c   5. d

Alternative Quiz 9-2A

A. (8 points: 2 points per item)
1. En rentrant à la maison, **j'ai eu un accident.**
2. J'ai **rencontré** une fille très sympa à la boum.
3. On a **rendez-vous** à la piscine à trois heures.
4. Samedi, on se promenait dans la forêt et on **s'est perdu**.

B. (6 points: 1 point per item)
1. est tombée en panne
2. privée de sortie
3. ne devineras jamais
4. Devine
5. a cassé
6. fait la tête

C. (16 points: 1 point per item)
1. faisait
2. avais
3. est tombée
4. se sont
5. n'ont pas voulu

6. ai dû
7. ai téléphoné
8. était
9. nous sommes disputés
10. a cassé
11. avons vu
12. faisait
13. ai parlé
14. avons décidé
15. n'avait pas
16. ai passé

Alternative Quiz 9-3A

A. (10 points: 2 points per item)
1. Pascale et Julie étaient en train de faire une promenade quand il a commencé à pleuvoir.
2. Tes parents étaient en train de regarder la télé quand il a commencé à pleuvoir.
3. J'étais en train de tondre le gazon quand il a commencé à pleuvoir.
4. Nous étions en train de prendre un bain de soleil quand il a commencé à pleuvoir.
5. Nicolas était en train de jouer au tennis quand il a commencé à pleuvoir.

B. (10 points: 2 points per item)
1. Je faisais une promenade quand j'ai vu un accident.
2. Je regardais la télé quand Valérie est arrivée.
3. Je travaillais au café quand j'ai rencontré une fille sympa.
4. Je montais l'escalier quand je suis tombé(e).
5. Je me lavais quand le téléphone a sonné.

C. (5 points: 1 point per item)
1. A propos
2. Heureusement
3. C'est-à-dire que / Malheureusement
4. Donc
5. À ce moment-la

D. (10 points: 2 points per item)
1. **a.** est tombé
2. **b.** étais
3. **b.** dormais
4. **b.** faisais
5. **c.** est tombée

Answers to Alternative Quizzes 10-1A, 10-2A, and 10-3A

Alternative Quiz 10-1A

A. (10 points: 2 points per item)
The advice will vary. These are the
beginnings only.
1. Dis-leur que...
2. Dis-lui que...
3. Explique-lui que...
4. Dis-lui que...
5. Ecris-lui...

B. (10 points: 1 point per item)
1. lui; un cadeau
2. Dis
3. Oublie
4. réconcilier
5. lui; pardon
6. Excuse
7. lui; ce qui

C. (8 points: 1 point per item)
1. Téléphone-lui ce soir.
2. Ne lui parle pas.
3. Explique-lui ce qui s'est passé.
4. Tu devrais l'oublier.
5. Invite-la à la boum.
6. Je dois leur demander pardon.
7. Tu dois nous expliquer ce qui s'est
   passé.
8. Je vais les inviter au cinéma.

D. (7 points: 1 point per item)
6; 3; 7; 2; 5; 1; 4

Alternative Quiz 10-2A

A. (5 points: 1 point per item)
Answers will vary.

B. (6 points: 2 points per item)
Possible answers:
1. Tu pourrais...
2. Ça t'ennuie de...
3. Ça t'embête de...

C. (12 points: 2 points per item)
Possible answers:
Robert : Bien sûr. / Avec plaisir. / Pas
de problème.
Sébastien : Désolé. / J'ai quelque chose
à faire. / C'est impossible.

D. (5 points: 1 point per item)
1. Non, je ne les ai pas fait.
2. Oui, je les ai envoyées.
3. Oui, je l'ai faite.
4. Oui, je l'ai sortie.
5. Non, je ne l'ai pas promené.

E. (7 points: 1 point per item)
1. **b.** la vaisselle
2. **a.** le cadeau
3. **a.** les paquets
4. **b.** les chiens
5. **a.** Ali
6. **b.** le disque
7. **c.** les sandwiches

Alternative Quiz 10-3A

A. (16 points: 2 points per item)
1. Désolé; m'en veux; grave
2. aurais pu; Excuse; pas de mal
3. ma faute; aurais dû

B. (8 points: 2 points per item)
Possible answers:
1. Ça ne fait rien.
2. Il n'y a pas de mal.
3. T'en fais pas.
4. C'est pas grave.

C. (6 points: 1 point per item)
1. J'aurais dû lui écrire.
2. J'aurais dû la faire.
3. J'aurais dû leur téléphoner.
4. J'aurais pu le sortir.
5. J'aurais dû les faire.
6. Je n'aurais pas dû la faire.

ANSWERS

Answers to Alternative Quizzes 11-1A, 11-2A, and 11-3A

Alternative Quiz 11-1A

A. (10 points: 2 points per item)
Possible answers:
1. C'est un groupe antillais.
2. C'est une chanteuse française.
3. C'est une chanson.
4. Elle est canadienne.
5. C'est chanteur.

B. (10 points: 2 points per item)
1. connais
2. connaît
3. connaissent
4. connaissez
5. connaissons

C. (10 points: 2 poins per item)
Possible answers:
1. le blues
2. le rock
3. le country
4. la musique classique
5. la musique antillaise

Alternative Quiz 11-2A

A. (12 points: 2 points per item)
1. Si on allait voir un film de science fiction.
2. Si on allait voir un film classique.
3. Si on allait voir un western.
4. Si on allait voir un film d'horreur.
5. Si on allait voir un film comique.
6. Si on allait voir un film d'amour.

B. (10 points: 2 points per item)
1. C'est un film comique.
2. C'est un film d'horreur.
3. C'est un film d'aventures.
4. C'est un film classique.
5. C'est un film d'amour.

C. (8 points: 2 points per item)
1. joue
2. à quelle heure
3. passe
4. qui

D. (5 points: 1 point per item)
1. **b.** à 13h 30.
2. **c.** Hercule.
3. **a.** À l'Odéon.
4. **c.** d'horreur.
5. **b.** Pierce Brosnan.

Alternative Quiz 11-3A

A. (10 points: 2 points per item)
1. que
2. qui
3. qu'
4. qui
5. qu'

B. (18 points: 3 points per item)
Possible answers:
Isabelle : C'est une belle histoire.
C'est une histoire passionnante.
Je te le recommande.
Bernard : Il n'y a pas d'histoire.
Ça casse pas des briques.
C'est bête.

C. (7 points: 1 point per item)
1. C'est une pièce de théâtre.
2. C'est un roman de science-fiction.
3. C'est un livre de poésie.
4. C'est un roman d'amour.
5. C'est une bande dessinée.
6. C'est une autobiographie.
7. C'est un roman policier.

Answers to Alternative Quizzes 12-1A, 12-2A, and 12-3A

Alternative Quiz 12-1A

A. (8 points: 1 point per item)
1. se trouve
2. au sud
3. Qu'est-ce qu'il y a
4. loups
5. renards
6. faire
7. faire du camping
8. faire une randonnée en raquettes

B. (15 points: 3 points per item)
1. Tes parents vont faire du vélo de montagne.
2. Tu vas faire du canotage.
3. Julie va faire une randonnée en raquettes.
4. Charles va faire une randonnée en skis.
5. Cédric va faire une randonnée pédestre.

C. (12 points: 2 points per item)
1. un canard
2. un raton laveur
3. un ours
4. une mouffette
5. un écureuil
6. un orignal

Alternative Quiz 12-2A

A. (8 points: 1 point per item)
1. peur
2. abandonne; Courage; crève de faim
3. fatigué; presque
4. meurs; n'en peux

B. (12 points: 2 points per item)
1. la lotion anti-moustiques
2. les allumettes
3. le sac de couchage
4. la boussole
5. la canne à pêche
6. la lampe de poche

C. (15 points: 3 points per item)
Possible answers:
1. Ne mutile pas les arbres.
2. Ne nourris pas les animaux.
3. Remporte les déchets. / Ne jette pas les déchets.
4. Respecte la nature.
5. Suit les sentier balisés.

Alternative Quiz 12-3A

A. (15 points: 1 point per item)
1. a fait
2. ai fait
3. nous sommes amusées
4. a décidé
5. s'est perdue
6. n'a pas suivi
7. était
8. avait
9. avait
10. ai fait
11. avons dormi
12. n'ai pas emporté
13. ai dû
14. a plu
15. ne suis pas allée

B. (10 points: 2 points per item)
1. Quand j'étais petit, j'écoutais toujours de la musique rock.
2. Je jouais au foot avec des amis.
3. J'ennuyais mes frères.
4. Je faisais souvent des bêtises.
5. Mes frères me taquinaient.

C. (5 points: 1 point per item)
4; 3; 5; 2; 1